LACTANTIUS AND MILTON

THIS VOLUME IS THE FIRST IN A SERIES
OF PUBLICATIONS BEGUN AT RADCLIFFE
COLLEGE IN THE SPRING OF 1929 IN CELE-
BRATION OF THE FIFTIETH ANNIVERSARY
OF THE FOUNDING OF THE COLLEGE

LONDON : HUMPHREY MILFORD

OXFORD UNIVERSITY PRESS

Lactantius and Milton

BY

KATHLEEN ELLEN HARTWELL

Cambridge, Massachusetts

HARVARD UNIVERSITY PRESS

1929

821
M662 Y
H337l

TO

MY BROTHER

PREFACE

THE original plan of this discussion was to treat the influence on Milton of all the Christian authors prescribed by Dean Colet for use in St. Paul's School, and to include a list of Milton's citations by name of all the Christian Fathers. However, the work on Lactantius alone proved sufficient; to study the rest of Colet's authors would have required more years than were at my disposal. Besides, the listing of Milton's patristic references was done in 1925 by Dr. Paul Pritchard, in his Cornell dissertation on the influence of Augustine on Milton, a work of which I have been glad to make use.

Insufficient knowledge of the Church Fathers other than Lactantius has been a constant hindrance to the evaluation of the influence of Lactantius himself. A wide knowledge of patristic literature would be necessary to pronounce definitely that such and such a passage can have been influenced by a single Father and by no other.

The point of departure for this book was the article, 'Milton as Schoolboy and Schoolmaster,' by Mr. A. F. Leach, read before the British Academy, December 10, 1908. He points out there certain evidences of an influence of Lactantius on Milton, without any attempt to go into the subject exhaustively, and states his belief that Milton's knowledge of the Church Father dated from his schoolboy days at St. Paul's. The aim of this discussion was to carry out more fully Mr. Leach's work, to determine Milton's knowledge of Lactantius and the extent of Lactantius' influence on Milton's poetry and prose. My hope to discover proof of an acquaintance with the Latin Father as early as St. Paul's days has not materialized.

The method has been a comparison of the works of both authors, by reading first in one and then in the other, with a constant sifting of the evidence with reference to a possible influence wherever thought or expression was similar. The first reading in Lactantius was done in the *Ante-Nicene Christian Library* translation of his works, but as soon as a salient point was reached, the translation was dropped for the original Latin, as edited by Brandt and Laubmann in the *Corpus Scriptorum*

Ecclesiasticorum Latinorum. The indices of Brandt and Miss Lockwood's *Lexicon to the English Poetical Works of John Milton* proved invaluable for tracking down sources in the one case and passages in Milton in the other. References to other Church Fathers come mostly from the index to Migne's *Patrology* and from Milton's own *Commonplace Book*, which should be the starting point for the study of patristic influence on him.

The results of this study are a general confirmation of Mr. Leach's theory. The entries in the *Commonplace Book* and the citations in the prose establish Milton's knowledge of and interest in Lactantius as a fact. To Mr. Leach's points are added six instances of a possible, or even probable influence of the Father upon the poet, one of which, occurring in *Comus*, gives 1634 as the earliest date supported by actual evidence for the use of Lactantius. With the examples of Lactantian influence presented by Mr. Leach, this book does not wholly agree, but it has attempted to prove that in general he is right, by producing evidence of the use of Lactantius by Milton in his prose and poetry, — Latin as well as English, — both early and late in his career.

My acknowledgments are many and varied, beginning with the staff of the Harvard College Library, more especially with Miss Reynolds, Miss Whitehead, and Mr. Briggs for their courtesy and assistance. For help on special questions, my thanks are due to Professors Lake and Wolfson. For valuable suggestions I am indebted to Professor Tatlock. And to Professor Lowes I owe more than I can express for his ready aid and his unfailing kindness and encouragement in the direction of this work.

K. E. H.

CONTENTS

I. MILTON'S ATTITUDE TOWARD THE FATHERS   3

II. LACTANTIUS IN THE *COMMONPLACE BOOK* .   18

III. LACTANTIUS IN THE *COMMENTARIES*   47

IV. OTHER EVIDENCES OF LACTANTIUS' INFLU-
ENCE IN THE WORKS OF MILTON   70

APPENDICES

A.   PASSAGES FROM LACTANTIUS SUMMARIZED
IN MILTON'S *COMMONPLACE BOOK*   137

B.   TITAN IN LACTANTIUS   147

C.   PURCHAS AND MILTON   150

D.   AZAZEL   158

E.   ST. PAUL'S SCHOOL   161

NOTES   167

BIBLIOGRAPHY   205

ABBREVIATIONS

ANCL	Ante-Nicene Christian Library.
CSEL	Corpus Scriptorum Ecclesiasticorum Latinorum.
Div. Insts.	Divinae Institutiones.
P. L.	Paradise Lost.
P. R.	Paradise Regained.
S. A.	Samson Agonistes.

'Quamvis et haec non satisfaciunt'

These words, in Milton's youthful hand, are his comment, in the *Commonplace Book*, on the argument of Lactantius that God deliberately permits evil.

There sounds a voice from this forgotten page
    That long ago Death silenced, yet again
    It speaks, unconscious of the ears of men,
The voice of Milton's youth to his ripe age.
Half pity, half reproach that olden sage
    Must find this tribute, for no faltering pen
    Was his who wrote here unafraid, 'Nay then,
No stream so parched my thirst could e'er assuage!'
Yet those young words, 'Non satisfaciunt,'
    Chime golden overtones — no weak despair
    Of utter truth to mar its splendid quest:
    'So, words of mine, seek that your perfect rest,
    The glory everlasting to declare —
Quamvis et haec non satisfaciunt!'

K. E. H.

I

MILTON'S ATTITUDE TOWARD
THE FATHERS

THE question of what poets read is one of perennial fascination, connected as it is with the problem, never wholly to be solved, of poetic inspiration. It would not be mere idle curiosity that would lead a student of literature to barter much in order to gain information as to any great poet's complete list of reading, for such knowledge would shed light on the nature of his genius. Such a discovery would help to show to what extent he drew on the treasuries of the past, as contained in books, and how far he drew simply and solely from that greatest open book, the world about him. In the case of John Milton, however, we have not far to seek in order to explore his reading. Few poets have been so obliging in bequeathing aids to research as was he, in leaving his *Commonplace Book*. To be sure, it was not given to the world until 1876, when the Historical Manuscripts Commission unearthed it among Sir F. Graham's papers, but since that time it has stood as a priceless record of Milton's thought and reading.

Of great significance are the entries in the *Commonplace Book* from the Greek and Latin Fathers of the Church. That Milton knew the Fathers is clear from the various references to them in the prose works; that he found them a stimulus to his thinking is shown by the *Commonplace Book*. They formed an important part of that background of enormous reading, as well as of arduous thinking, that lay behind *Paradise Lost*, *Paradise Regained*, and the various prose works on ecclesiastical subjects. The Bible itself was his prime authority and inspiration,[1] but that was not the age and Milton was not the man to overlook the contributions to Christian thought made by the Fathers of the Church.

Milton's own strong intellectual curiosity, his longing for ever more knowledge of 'the best and honourablest things,'[2] would have been quite sufficient grounds for his interest in the Fathers, but it must be added that he lived in a day when they were in the scholarly fashion. Ecclesiastical controversies, which then waxed so hot, could hardly have been maintained without extensive quotation of the Fathers: if you did not refer to them, your opponent did, thereby scoring a point. An excellent example of how far one could go in this 'paroxysm of citations,'[3] to use Milton's own words, is furnished by Archbishop Laud's conference[4] with 'Mr. Fisher the Jesuit.'[5] This conference was held by order of James I, on May 24, 1622, before 'the lord marquess Buckingham, and the Countess, his mother,'[6] ostensibly to win back the Countess from Catholicism, but really to settle the mind of Buckingham himself, who was wavering in his religious convictions.[7] The Archbishop buttresses his arguments against Catholicism with direct citations from no less than fifteen Fathers, both Greek and Latin: Ambrose,[8] Athanasius,[9] Augustine,[10] Basil,[11] Chrysostom,[12] Cyprian,[13] Cyril of Alexandria,[14] Epiphanius,[15] Gregory Nazianzen,[16] Gregory of Nyssa,[17] Irenaeus,[18] Jerome,[19] Lactantius,[20] Origen,[21] and Tertullian.[22] Nor does this list include such names as Hilary,[23] John of Damascus,[24] Justin Martyr,[25] or Minucius Felix,[26] who are, however, cited in Laud's footnotes. It does not appear that the lady altered her belief under this bombardment of authorities, but the fact remains that contenders on any side in the religious controversies of

Milton's time tried to marshal an array of Church Fathers as heavy artillery, to back up the charge made by means of texts from Scripture.

Milton himself, whose direct patristic references are scattered throughout his prose works, even in the political tracts,[27] does not treat the Fathers as a uniform body, to be regarded with anything like unvarying and unquestioning respect. He may use them as weapons against themselves: 'The ancientest and best of the fathers have disclaimed all sufficiency in themselves that men should rely on, and sent all comers to the scriptures, as all-sufficient.'[28] He may speak of the Fathers with downright scorn, as he does in *Of Reformation:* 'Who is ignorant of the foul errors, the ridiculous wresting of Scripture, the heresies, the vanities thick sown through the volumes of Justin Martyr, Clemens, Origen, Tertullian, and others of eldest time?'[29] Or again, Milton may rebut fiercely the patristic arguments of his adversaries, in any one of various ways that have already been discussed by Dr. Paul Pritchard, in his dissertation on the influence of Augustine on Milton.[30] Briefly to summarize these methods of attack, Milton saw that he could impugn the credibility of his opponents'

citations by showing the text to be dubious, or
even corrupt, as in the case of Ignatius;[31] by prov-
ing certain attributions to be spurious, such as
some of the epistles of Ignatius;[32] by demonstrating
that the writer was unable to give an accurate re-
port, as was the youthful Irenaeus;[33] or by pointing
out that certain patristic statements were contrary
to Scripture.[34] Perhaps the most concise statement
of the case against the Fathers is to be found in
Of Reformation, where Milton sums up his reasons
for not accepting patristic evidence without due ex-
amination: 'A threefold corruption . . . will be found
upon them [i.e. 'those ancient times']. 1. The best
times were spreadingly infected. 2. The best men
of those times foully tainted. 3. The best writings
of those men dangerously adulterated.'[35] This is a
severe and a sweeping statement, one that few
men of Milton's time would have had the scholarly
audacity to make; does it mean that Milton had
no use whatever for the Fathers, or that he never
drew upon them to back up his arguments?

Before one looks for an answer to this question,
one should recall the circumstances under which
he wrote the anti-episcopal works, where his most
direct attacks on the authority of the Fathers

occur. In *Of Reformation*, for example, Milton was doing something more than answer Bishop Hall's 'Humble Remonstrance,' a pamphlet which was, on the whole, of a conciliatory tone.[36] But Milton would have none of conciliation or condescension, for with all the intensity of his nature and all the powers of his rhetoric he was flinging himself into the struggle between the Episcopal and Presbyterian parties. Wanting his Reformation all at once and unqualified, he came to hate its hinderers, one group of whom he called the 'Antiquitarians,' who loved bishops, as he scornfully said, as they would old coins, 'for antiquity's sake.' [37] This controversial bitterness, so characteristic of Milton's time, would to-day be regarded as a blemish on his judgment. It must, however, be remembered that these pamphlets on the Church were written in a day when ecclesiastical controversy was no mere armchair debate, but when it had its very grim side. It was a time when Milton could well ask of the Laudian party, 'What numbers of faithful and freeborn Englishmen, and good Christians, have been constrained to forsake their dearest home, their friends and kindred, whom nothing but the wide ocean, and the savage deserts of America, could hide and shelter from the fury of the bishops?' [38]

Feeling as deeply as he did, then, Milton gave absolutely no quarter to his foes in argument. As Dr. Hale says, he was 'on the alert to seize every fact to confute those he considered in league with the devil,' [39] and often the use of the Fathers was a vulnerable point in the arguments of these opponents he so detested. It may be that some of the heat of conflict was introduced from his views on his adversaries into his remarks on their authorities, since in no others of his prose works does he assail the Fathers with such violence, but apparently it is sometimes his opponents' way of handling patristic evidence with which he feels impatience, rather than with the Fathers themselves. Milton, with his wide acquaintance with 'the legitimate writings of the fathers,' [40] was the last person to be impressed by a random show of patristic texts, just as, with his characteristic lack of regard for authority just because it was authority, he was not to be overwhelmed in argument by the mere bandying of citations, uttered with a blind trust in the efficacy of the great names of the Fathers. This uncritical acceptance of everything patristic is the object of his sarcasm in *The Reason of Church Government Urged against Prelaty*, where Milton speaks of himself as being

> put from beholding the bright countenance of truth in the quiet and still air of delightful studies, to come into the dim reflection of hollow antiquities sold by the seeming bulk, and there be fain to club quotations with men whose learning and belief lies in marginal stuffings, who, when they have, like good sumpters, laid ye down their horse-loads of citations and fathers at your door, with a rhapsody of who and who were bishops here or there, ye may take off their packsaddles, their day's work is done, and episcopacy, as they think, stoutly vindicated.[41]

This superior knowledge of Church literature, as Dr. Pritchard has pointed out,[42] was in several instances a most effective weapon in Milton's hands, for there were times when he could cite the same Fathers who had been misinterpreted by his opponents as giving actual evidence for his side. Again it is the undiscriminating use of patristic works and reliance upon their mere antiquity that Milton would seem to be attacking when he says, 'Whatsoever time, or the heedless hand of blind chance, hath drawn down from of old to this present, in her huge drag-net, whether fish or sea-weed, shells or shrubs, unpicked, unchosen, those are the fathers.' [43] The implication is that analysis and careful choice will discover something of worth in this unsifted mass, which his antagonists accepted as a uniformly valuable whole.

This implication becomes explicit farther on in the same pamphlet, in a passage where Milton seems to be making a judicious statement of his position in regard to the Fathers. It is, he says, 'the part of a well-learned man to have read diligently the ancient fathers of the church, and to be no stranger in the volumes of the fathers,' in order that he may be able to recognize what survives of primitive truth and to refute the arguments of those 'who willingly pass by that which is orthodoxal in them, and studiously cull out that which is commentitious, and best for their turns, not weighing the fathers in the balance of scripture, but scripture in the balance of the fathers.' [44]

Milton realized that the names of the Fathers were often used merely to impress the unlearned. 'Pomp and ostentation of reading,' he says in *A Treatise of Civil Power in Ecclesiastical Causes*,[45] 'is admired among the vulgar; but doubtless, in matters of religion, he is learnedest who is plainest.' Again, alluding to his ecclesiastical opponents' references to Church councils, so often linked with quotations from the Fathers, he warns his readers not to be deceived 'by men that would overawe your ears with big names and huge tomes that contradict and repeal one another, because they can cram a margin with citations. Do but winnow their chaff from their wheat, ye shall see their great heap shrink and wax thin, past belief.' [46] This unthinking acceptance of patristic authority is what Milton is objecting to, when, in *Animadversions upon the Remonstrant's Defence against Smectymnuus*, he speaks of the 'overawful esteem of those more ancient than trusty fathers, whom custom and fond opinion, weak principles, and the neglect of sounder and superior knowledge hath exalted so high as to have gained them a blind reverence.' [47]

But Milton has a good word to say for the Fathers, when the acrimony of debate is forgotten. In *Tetrachordon*, he prefaces his extensive quotations from the Fathers with these words:

This opinion which I bring, hath been favoured, and by some of those affirmed, who in their time were able to carry what they taught, had they urged it, through all Christendom; or to have left it such a credit with all good men, as they who could not boldly use the opinion, would have feared to censure it. . . . It will be enough for me to find, that the thoughts of wisest heads heretofore, and hearts no less reverenced for devotion, have tended this way, and contributed their lot in some good measure towards this which hath been here attained.[48]

Again, he calls the age of Justin Martyr 'those pure and next to apostolic times.' [49] With reference to the time of Constantine, and therefore of Lactantius, he says, 'And this was an age of the church, both ancient and cried up still for the most flourishing in knowledge and pious government since the apostles.' [50] In this same work, he refers to the Fathers whom he has cited as authorities, as 'all these ancient and great asserters.' [51] What can have been the reason for this right-about-face? Milton is not a man to be lightly accused of disingenuousness, and there are other more probable explanations. Either he must have altered his attitude toward the general authority of the Fathers, as he continued the study of them beyond the days of the Presbyterian controversy, or, as seems more likely, he found that there was much good that he could honestly say of them, when he came to regard them as allies, rather than as the pawns of his antagonists. It could hardly be maintained, however, that Milton's previous attitude toward the Fathers helps his case when he comes to make his own use of them in *Tetrachordon*.

His statements, then, about the Fathers and their authority must be taken as a whole, whether they are attacks made in the heat of strife, citations used to prove his own point, or mere passing references scattered through the body of his work. Always holding the essence of Protestant doctrine, he invariably names the Bible as the fountainhead of religious truth, but he also believed that there was profit to be derived from a study of the Fathers. A wise use of the good to be found in them, he declares in *Of Prelatical Episcopacy*, taken together with the Gospel itself, is a means of mastering false doctrine, but to 'turn this our discreet and wary usage of them into a blind devotion towards them'[52] means to Milton to slide back into an acceptance of antiquity that would be a denial of the principles of Reformation. His position is, then, that the Bible should come before the Fathers, and a long way before them, and that acceptance of them, like the married state, is not to be entered into unadvisedly or lightly, but discreetly, advisedly, soberly.

Much work remains to be done before Milton's debt to each of the individual Fathers can be determined. Dr. Pritchard has already covered the ground of Milton's direct quotations from the body of Fathers as a whole, and he has also shown that Milton knew and used extensively the works of Augustine, weaving his ideas into the very warp and woof of *Paradise Lost*, as well as into the tracts on divorce, the *De Doctrina Christiana*, and the works defending the execution of Charles I. In general, Dr. Pritchard seems to have established his case admirably, but he has laid himself open to criticism in his statement that Milton was inaccurate in two particulars: 'at least one instance of misquotation appears in his discussion of Ignatius, and another instance of a mistaken reference in the case of Justin Martyr, whose *Second Apology* he refers to as if it were the *First*.' [53]

The apparent misquotation of Ignatius occurs in the passage in *Of Reformation* where 'the ancientest of the extant fathers' is quoted as saying, in the *Epistle to the Philadelphians*, that 'it belongs to them as to the church of God to choose a bishop.' [54] Dr. Pritchard accuses Milton of inaccuracy for not using the word 'deacon' here, and supposes that

the mistake is due to haste in writing and conse-
quent failure to verify the reference.[55] What looks
like a slip, however, is due merely to the fact that
there are two disputed groups of the epistles of
Ignatius, the long and the short recensions, not to
mention the Curetonian recension, which is not
here involved.[56] The reading of the long recension
is ἐπίσκοπον, that of the short recension διάκονον.
Migne gives both the readings, the former in
Epistolae Interpolatae,[57] the latter in *Epistolae Ge-
nuinae*.[58] There was but one version, however,
available to Milton in a printed text at the time
when he was writing *Of Reformation*, since the short,
or Vossian, recension was not published until five
years later, in 1646. The possibility of his having
used a manuscript based on the Medicean one at
Florence is banished by Professor Hanford's identi-
fication of the edition of Ignatius quoted in Milton's *Commonplace Book* as that of Geneva, 1623.[59]
Milton, accordingly, did use a printed text, and the
reading of that edition, as of all other editions in
1641, is, by actual verification, ἐπίσκοπον, whereby
Milton's accuracy is justified.

The alleged mistake in the numbering of the
Apologies of Justin Martyr is another example of

a difference in usage between editions. To-day the *Apology* of sixty-eight chapters, addressed to Antoninus Pius, is numbered *First*, while that of fifteen chapters, addressed to the Roman senate, is made *Second*. This is an exact reversal of the procedure in the earliest extant manuscript,[60] where our *First Apology* is numbered *Second*. The example of the manuscript was followed until the edition of Maranus in 1742.[61] Accordingly, it was impossible for Milton to refer to what we call the *Second Apology* in any other way than as if it were our *First*. It is not necessary to track down the edition he used, that of Cologne, 1636,[62] to establish his accuracy once more, since no edition of his time bore any other numbering.

With the bulk of general patristic quotations already handled by Dr. Pritchard, the purpose of this discussion is to determine the extent to which Milton drew on Lactantius, for ideas or for expressions, in the hope of shedding more light on the larger question of Milton's attitude toward and his use of the Fathers.

II

LACTANTIUS IN THE "COMMON-PLACE BOOK"

THAT Milton was intimately acquainted with the works of Lactantius is attested by seven entries in the *Commonplace Book* [1] and two explicit citations in the prose. [2] Most of these citations are naturally from the *Divine Institutes*, two coming from the second book, four from different parts of the sixth, and one from the seventh, but there is also one quotation each from the shorter works, the *De Ira Dei* and the *De Opificio Dei*. Such a wide range of citation, with no correspondence between the jottings in the notebook and the references in the prose, would seem to contribute towards the general body of evidence which shows that Milton had little in common with that class of pseudo-scholars he so looked down upon, 'that pretend to be great rabbies in these studies,' but who have 'scarce saluted them from the strings, and the titlepage; or . . . have been but the ferrets and mousehunts of an index' [3] — a passage which, by the way, is recommended to the notice of those who insist that Milton was constitutionally incapable of any brand of humor.

Masson, however, does not give him credit for thoroughgoing patristic scholarship, but thinks that 'doubtless some of his readings in the Fathers were but researches for the occasion *in locis citatis* after he had Usher's tract in his hand.'[4] The entries in the *Commonplace Book* from certain of the Fathers in question may help us to test this supposition, since, if Milton were reading Church literature with an eye only to its immediate usefulness in controversy, what would be more natural than that he should make note of references to the disputed points in his notebook? (Of course, one must take into consideration that he may not have wanted to enter these facts of only passing interest in his volume of memorabilia, and may have recorded them in some more temporary way. But, in that case, the entries in the *Commonplace Book* would be proof in themselves that Milton was reading with a purpose beyond merely answering Archbishop Usher.) Now, of the patristic authorities cited by Usher in *The Judgment of Doctor Rainoldes touching the originall of Episcopacy*,[5] the

tract to which Masson is referring, four are to be
found in the *Commonplace Book*, in Usher's pamphlet, and in *Of Prelatical Episcopacy*, which was
Milton's answer. These four Fathers are Eusebius,
Tertullian, Ignatius, and Clement of Alexandria.
Eusebius may be omitted from this comparison
from the start, since Professor Hanford has shown,
on the basis of handwriting, that the entries from
Eusebius are all of a group dated before 1639,[6]
while Usher's tract was not published until 1641.
Of course, if a comparison of the other three
Fathers mentioned in both Usher and the *Commonplace Book* shows a marked coincidence, the conclusion would be that Milton was reading these
particular Fathers for their immediately practical
application to the purposes of discussion. However, a glance at the table in the notes [7] will show
that there is not the shadow of a resemblance between the two sets of references, and Masson's
statement is at least not borne out. It will be
shown later [8] that Milton's greatest biographer did
not always verify his references. Another point in
favor of Milton's disinterested reading is brought
out by Dr. Pritchard.[9] Milton, in several instances,
does not mention page or chapter for the passage

in question; Dr. Pritchard remarks that Milton
would have been precise in his references, if he had
been recording these passages only as ammunition
against his adversaries.

But, to return to Milton and Lactantius, there
is no doubt of the exactness of the references here,
for book and chapter are always cited. The first
appearance of Lactantius is on the fourth page of
the *Index Ethicus*, under the heading '*Malum
morale.*' The problem of evil is evidently troubling
Milton here. 'Why,' he asks, 'does God allow
evil?' After a reference to Tertullian's *De Spectaculis*,[10] the second entry on the page reads,

Cur permittit deus malum? ut ratio virtuti constare
possit. virtus enim malo arguitur, illustratur, exercetur,
quemadmodum disserit *Lactantius*, l. 5, c. 7, ut haberet
ratio et prudentia in quo se exerceret, eligendo bona,
fugiendo mala. *Lactan.* de ira dei, c. 13, quamvis et
haec non satisfaciunt.

There is a slip here, whether of the pen or of the
memory, which is quite unlike Milton's usual accuracy, in the words *ut ratio virtuti constare possit*,
which are in Lactantius *ut ratio virtutis constare
posset*. A search through nineteen editions of Lactantius [11] fails to disclose Milton's version. The

entry as a whole is a summary of part of the seventh chapter of the fifth book of Lactantius; only the single phrase mentioned, with the probably remembered word *exercetur*, is taken from the original. Since so few words are borrowed from the whole chapter, it appears that Milton was here quoting from memory, and that his memory played him false. This method of quotation is in line with what Professor Hanford says of the usual way of work in the *Commonplace Book*, that Milton did not 'ordinarily . . . use it for materials gathered in the immediate process of research, but rather as a permanent aid to his thought and memory. . . . The method employed was apparently to mark the significant passages and from time to time to write up a series of notes based on them under appropriate headings.' [12]

It is interesting to see that Milton must have written the previous entry on the page with his volume of Tertullian open, from the literal exactness with which he quotes him.[13] One might be led to assume that Milton remembered the passage from Lactantius while he was copying the one from Tertullian, had not Professor Hanford pointed out that 'close inspection of the writing will show that in both cases (pages 4 and 241) the Lactantius entry belongs to a later stratum.' [14] The citations from Tertullian, according to Professor Hanford, were written at a transitional stage in Milton's handwriting, when he used sometimes the Greek and sometimes the Italic 'e,' while the entries on Lactantius are characterized by the uniform use of the Italic 'e.' [15] This means that the Lactantius entries were written after the journey to Italy (1638–39).[16]

The part of the chapter in the *Divine Institutes* that Milton is summarizing in his first entry deals with the problem of evil in a thoroughly assured manner.[17] Lactantius does not say that God actually created evil, but that He purposely did not abolish it, in order that virtue might be brought to the test. Indeed, the chapter makes the resistance of evil and vice the very definition of virtue, so that, without its opposite, virtue could not exist. Evil, then, is part of God's deliberate choice for man's spiritual environment, a necessity for the very existence of the moral nature. This is one of the favorite ideas of Lactantius, and in its emphasis on the combating of evil it is like Milton's own conception of militant virtue.

The chapter mentioned from the *De Ira Dei* introduces the same idea, this time in connection with wisdom.[18] This faculty, Lactantius says, distinguishes man, making him the rational animal, the consummation of divine handiwork, but wisdom is maintained only by the constant choice between good and evil. Wisdom could not exist without evil from which to choose the good, and the removal of evil would do away with wisdom, as with virtue. So far the argument is well handled, but there is a point where Lactantius is guilty of arguing in a circle. Immediately after his proof that evil is a necessary condition for the practice of wisdom, which, as Lactantius conceives it, is the choice of the best, he turns in his tracks and states that we need wisdom for the detection of evil. Could this flaw in Lactantius' thought escape Milton's keen eye? And could he be satisfied with such a conception of God, based on the expediency of accounting for evil? The answer is not far to seek, for after the reference to this chapter comes one of Milton's rare passing comments, the more precious for its rarity: 'quamvis et haec non satisfaciunt.' For not even these high-sounding words could satisfy Milton; not even the Church Fathers could be allowed to do his thinking for him.

The latter part of the chapter in the *De Ira Dei*
applies this same principle, of God's retention of
evil in the scheme of things, to an ingenious argument put forward by Epicurus, who was Lactantius' *bête noire*. To quote the translation from the
Ante-Nicene Christian Library, 'God either wishes
to take away evils, and is unable; or He is able,
and is unwilling; or He is neither willing nor able;
or he is both willing and able.'[19] Epicurus here puts
the question in such a way as to strain either one's
faith or one's logic, for a willing and unable God
would be impotent, and therefore not God; an able
and unwilling God would be envious; unable and
unwilling, He would be both impotent and envious; or both able and willing — then whence
comes evil? Lactantius spikes the enemy's guns
by accepting one of Epicurus' premises: God, according to the Christian Father, is able, though unwilling, to do away with evil. Yet, so far from
being envious, He is thereby bestowing on man the
means to that very wisdom which has for its goal
immortality, through the knowledge of God. But
even this clever answer to the verbal fencings of
Epicurus could not satisfy Milton's craving for ul-
timate wisdom: 'quamvis et haec non satisfaciunt.'

In the first sentence of the first passage that
Milton cites from the *Divine Institutes*, Lactantius
refers to other places where he touches on the same
main idea, that virtue exists only through use
against an adversary. When he says that he has
already declared this doctrine in another place,[20]
he is probably referring to the twenty-ninth chapter of the third book, the first place where he de-
velops this argument at length. Here he states
that God did not consign Satan to immediate punishment at the time of the primal transgression,
because, without Satan's temptation, man would
lack the means of strengthening and perfecting his
virtue.[21] There are also a number of other passages
that seek to prove that virtue is based on opposition.[22] It is noteworthy that the greatest number
of passages in any one book is the four from the
sixth book, from which also Milton drew the largest
number of his own citations in the *Commonplace
Book*. Although he quotes only one of these passages, it is probable that he had read them all, for
that the whole of Lactantius was known to Milton
would seem to be proved by the wide range of his
various citations, by his natural interest in the Lactantian material and arguments, and by the ac-

curacy and thoroughness of his habits of reading, which could hardly leave him satisfied with a smattering of such an author.

It is not necessary to discuss in detail each of the passages in which Lactantius, treating of beleaguered virtue, handles this, his jewel of an idea, letting the light of it flash from first one facet and then another. There seems, however, to be a connection between several of these passages and the *Areopagitica*, in which Milton makes the necessity of the opposition of vice to virtue one of the basic ideas.[23] Most striking is that ringing sentence which begins, 'I cannot praise a fugitive and cloistered virtue,' which may well be the poet's way of putting an idea that may first have flashed into his mind from the pages of Lactantius. That this is not wholly a matter of guess is shown by Milton's own entry in the *Commonplace Book*, where he puts into words of his own the fundamental thought of the chapter from the fifth book of the *Divine Institutes*. If that thought had been the merest commonplace to him, would he have taken the trouble to elaborate it in this entry?

Between the sentence in the *Areopagitica* and the fourth-century Latin are certain 'hooks-and-eyes

of the memory' which may serve to connect the
two. In the note already discussed from the *Commonplace Book*, Milton repeats one word, using both
the forms *exercetur* and *exerceret*, a word which
finds its echo in the *Areopagitica:* 'I cannot praise
a fugitive and cloistered virtue, *unexercised* and
unbreathed.' Here there is a heightening of effect
that comes with the passion Milton felt for his
threatened ideal of liberty, and the word comes to
life that had lain dormant in the note. But that is
not all, for the word is a favorite with Lactantius
for use in just the same general connection.[24] No-
tably, he uses it in the very chapter Milton was
summarizing in his note, just two sentences before
the phrase that Milton recalled specifically. What,
then, may have been the steps between the passage
in Lactantius and Milton's great declaration of the
strenuousness of virtue? The *Commonplace Book*,
of course, is the connecting link, for the chances
are that Milton, when he twice employed forms of
the verb *exercere* was, whether consciously or un-
consciously, influenced by Lactantius' use of the
form *exerceatur* as the climax of the sentence just
previous to 'ut ratio virtutis constare posset,' the
words that Milton surely recalled.[25] Then, in

writing the *Areopagitica*, when he came to a defence of the idea of virtue militant, what would be more natural than that the word 'unexercised' should flash into his mind unbidden, bringing with it close-packed associations, perhaps not even recognized? Or there may have been actually defined the heartening memory that, back in the fourth century after Christ, one of the leaders of Christian thought had shared this ideal. Not for a minute is there any question of Milton's being any the less a creative genius because he may possibly, or even probably, have recalled from his reading one of Lactantius' favorite words. Milton puts it to his own uses, and it shines anew, as it never shone in any setting Lactantius gave it. Nor is there any supposition that Milton was incapable of writing this passage had he never laid eyes on Lactantius. But the fact is that he *had* read the Latin Father, and that he had been enough impressed to enter the words of Lactantius in the *Commonplace Book*. Milton is not the poorer, but the richer for the host of recognized or unrecognized associations with which the fourth-century apologist acted as a bulwark to the seventeenth-century poet's ideal of virtue.

Can we go a step further and find some one of
those associations which may have been raised in
Milton's use of the word 'unexercised'? It seems
possible, since there is still another word to be
found in the *Areopagitica* which is also popular
with Lactantius, and that one is 'adversary,' in
'that never sallies out and seeks her adversary.' [26]
It is a word that Lactantius connects with the idea
of virtue even more often than *exercere*.[27] The sixth
book of the *Divine Institutes*, which Milton must
have known well, because of his four entries from
it in his *Commonplace Book*, has two separate passages that connect 'adversary' with virtue, but
even more significant is the passage already mentioned in the twenty-ninth chapter of the third
book. Here, within successive sentences, Lactantius uses both the test words *exerceat* and *aduersarius*. He is here explaining why Satan was not at
once given over to condign punishment, and says:

idcirco enim in primordiis transgressionis non statim ad
poenam detrusus a deo est, ut hominem malitia sua
exerceat ad uirtutem: quae nisi agitetur, nisi uexatione
adsidua roboretur, non potest esse perfecta, siquidem
uirtus est perferendorum malorum fortis et inuicta
patientia. ex quo fit ut uirtus nulla sit, si *aduersarius*
desit.[28]

And again, a few sentences farther on, the same idea has its groove deepened in the reader's memory by two repetitions of the crucial word: 'sed ut *aduersarium* suum nesciunt, sic ne uirtutem quidem sciunt, cuius scientia ab *aduersarii* notione descendit.' [29] Here we have another stage to add to the progress of the thought from Lactantius to the *Areopagitica*. The seventh chapter of the fifth book of the *Divine Institutes* stimulated Milton to enter a note in his *Commonplace Book*, where he uses the words *exercetur* and *exerceretur*. A glance at this entry might have roused in Milton's mind the memory of another passage on the self-same theme, that is, the twenty-ninth chapter of the third book. And here *exerceat* is found, associated, though not contiguously, with another favorite word, *adversarius*, which is further impressed on the memory by two repetitions a few sentences farther on. Virtue to be exercised against an adversary — that is the Lactantian pattern, and also the pattern of the sentence in the *Areopagitica*, although Milton need not have specifically remembered the patristic original. His unconscious recollection might well have been sufficient to have made Lactantius operative in Milton's most famous pamphlet.

An interesting problem is presented by the twenty-second chapter of the fifth book, where *exerceat* and *adversarius* again occur, but this time separated by seven sentences. The chances for association are, of course, considerably less in this instance. Furthermore, *exercet* is here found, not in Lactantius' own words, but in a quotation from Seneca, and the question immediately arises, whether Milton may not have been influenced by Seneca, rather than by Lactantius. The whole passage in Seneca's *De Providentia* must give us pause, for here, within nine sentences, occur the words *exercitationes*, *exerceantur*, and *adversario*, all connected with the thought of virtue.[30] Does this upset the conclusion that Milton's conception of virtue in the *Areopagitica* was colored by Lactantian associations? The main argument for the adoption of the idea from Seneca rests on his classical priority; Milton might certainly have drawn directly from the fountainhead of the classics themselves, rather than from the intermediate Church Father. Or, since Seneca was probably the source for Lactantius on this point, as has been remarked by the most recent editors of that Father,[31] one might maintain that Milton's memories of the pas-

sage in Seneca were revived by running across
the quotation of it in Lactantius. This may have
been true, without canceling the previous conclusion, that Lactantius was here operative in the
work of Milton. In the first place, the thought in
its most characteristic form in Lactantius is re-
peatedly couched in military terms, of generals and
soldiers, enemies and expeditions, that are at least
hinted at in Milton's 'that sallies not out and seeks
her adversary,' and in 'the true warfaring Christian' of the previous sentence.[32] There is none of
this coloring in the passage in Seneca. The frequent
reiteration of the thought in Lactantius, until it
becomes a pattern, would make it probable that
Milton, when he glanced at the note in his *Commonplace Book*, recalled these repetitions, if, as we
assume, he had once read them. Even though he
may have remembered his Seneca, he would not
have forgotten his Lactantius. But the most co-
gent reason for maintaining that it was Lactantius who lay behind the sentence in the *Areopagitica* is one of Milton's own offering, namely, the
entry in the *Commonplace Book*, which shows that
it was Lactantius, rather than Seneca, that Milton
wanted to remember as having said something

noteworthy about the strenuousness of virtue. Instead, therefore, of subtracting Lactantius from the complex of impressions that brought forth the sentence under consideration, we have but to add Seneca, probably as a less rather than a more important remembrance.

Of the rest of the entries on Lactantius in the *Commonplace Book,* no other presents such complications. The next note,[33] under the heading '*De Viro Bono,*' deals with the question of why an upright and just man who is unwilling to avenge himself for wrong done him should be content to put up with an appearance of poor spirit. 'Cur viri boni et alioquin egregii inertis ut plurimum et pusilli animi speciem prae se ferunt, primoque intuitu nullius esse pretii videntur, respondet *Lactantius* ut haberent unde summam virtutem patientiam possent quotidiè exercere, l. 6, c. 18.' This is a question that, at some time in his career, might well have beset 'the Lady of Christ's.' Two other entries follow on the same page, one from Chrysostom, which Professor Hanford declares to be of uncertain date, although it may be contemporaneous with the Lactantius note,[34] and one from an Italian history, in the hand which Professor Han-

ford calls that of Amanuensis F,[35] thus dating the
entry as having been made during the period of
Milton's partial or total blindness. These latter
notes need not concern us. Lactantius' answer to
Milton's question is merely summarized in brief;
there is no reproduction of the actual patristic language, except in the word *inertis* and in the inevitable *virtutem* and *patientiam*.[36]

The fourth entry from Lactantius occurs under
the heading *De Libidine*, and deals with the subject
of paederasty: 'Παιδεραsία seu ἀρρενοκοττια. Quid
potest esse sanctum iis qui aetatem imbecillam et
praesidio indigentem libidini suae depopulandum
foedandamque prostraverint. *Lactant.* l. 6, c. 23.' [37]
This note is significant in showing that 'the Lady
of Christ's' did not hesitate to call a spade a spade,
and that he had read with close attention this very
plain-spoken chapter in Lactantius. The note is
quoted *verbatim et literatim* from the twenty-third
chapter of the sixth book of the *Divine Institutes*,[38]
except that Milton writes *prostraverint*, where every
edition in the Harvard University Library reads
substraverint. This may be a slip of the pen, a
minor inaccuracy due to the haste of writing, or it
is not impossibly a different reading in Milton's own

edition of Lactantius, which has not yet been identified. This note from Lactantius, according to
Professor Hanford, was written at the same time
as the succeeding note on the sodomy of King
Mempricius,[39] recollected from the reading of Geoffrey of Monmouth in the Horton period.[40] This
latter entry, referring as it does to a very brief
statement in Geoffrey,[41] shows how Milton's memory had retained for several years the barest record
of a fact from his reading. This same detail is repeated, many years later, in *The History of Britain*.[42]

The first entry on page eighteen of the *Commonplace Book* is concerned with the question, 'Wherein
lies human strength?' and summarizes the third
chapter of Lactantius' *De Opificio Dei*. The main
argument of this chapter is the superiority of human wisdom over brute strength, and Milton sums
the matter up neatly in his note:

Fortitudo hominis non in corpore sed in ratione, quae
firmissimum hominis praesidium et munimentum est,
consistit. quod hinc liquet hominem hoc solo rationis
adminiculo etiam in robustissima quaeque animalia
dominari, et nocere posse, si libet. *Lactant*. de opif. dei,
c. 3.[43]

The other notes on the page are not contemporaneous[44] or significant for us. The chapter from Lac-

tantius is one of his most striking,[45] meeting, as it
does in a masterly way, the arraignment of Nature
by Lucretius, for having made man inferior to
other animals in his physical equipment.[46] Against
the idea that man's defenceless state at birth and
his prolonged period of helplessness are arguments
that Nature favors the lower animals rather than
man, Lactantius cites the laborious rearing of
birds. But his main answer is that Nature has
actually bestowed much more on man than on the
beasts of the field in the single gift of reason. Physical inferiority and all, man is really better equipped
than other animals, since by his wisdom he can
subdue even the most powerful of them to his authority. The note on this chapter by Milton is
another of his summaries, independent of the original in phrasing, except for *munimentum* and the
word *ratione*, which is too obviously required by
the sense to show reminiscence.

The next entry on Lactantius occurs in the *Index
Politicus*, under the heading '*Amor in patriam*.' [47]
This time it is a quite different kind of fillip that
Lactantius has given to Milton's thought, from
the sixth chapter of the sixth book of the *Divine
Institutes:* [48]

Virtus ista cautè a philosophis petenda est, non enim caecus et carnalis patriae amor ad rapinas, et caedes, et odium vicinatum gentium rapere nos debet, ut patriam imperio, opibus, aut gloriâ augeamus; sic enim ethnici fecerunt; Christianos autem inter se pacem colere oportet, et non appetere aliena: hanc ob causam invehitur in philosophiam *Lactantius*, l. 6, c. 6.

Later than this entry is the one below it from Holinshed.[49] In the note from Lactantius, the only possible reminiscences of the original wording are to be found in the not especially significant words *imperio* and *augeamus*. The chief interest in this passage is to see the intensely nationalistic Milton considering the virtue of being internationally minded.

The final note on Lactantius, also in the *Index Politicus*,[50] is a later addition to a long entry on Tertullian's *De Spectaculis*.[51] The entry on Lactantius reads:

Et *Lactantius*, l. 6, c. 20, argumentis nihilo firmioribus rem scenicam universam in vitio ponit: nec semel quidem cogitasse videtur, corruptelas quidem theatricas meritò tolli debere, omnem autem idcirco rerum dramaticarum usum penitus aboleri nihil necesse esse, immo potius nimis insulsum esset; quid enim in totâ philosophiâ aut gravius aut sanctius aut sublimius tragaedia recte constitutâ; quid utilius ad humanae vitae casus et conversiones uno intuitu spectandos? idem etiam capite sequenti totam artem musicam videtur e medio sublatam velle.

The connection between the two notes is, of course, the patristic condemnation of the drama, an attack which Milton resented and which he answered with spirit, in his comment on Lactantius. As a substitute for the Roman games and shows of which the Fathers so disapproved, Tertullian proposed to the Christian the contemplation of great spiritual events, such as the coming of Christ and the approaching Judgment, in words that caught Milton's attention.[52] Not often in the *Commonplace Book* do we find such a comment as he makes here on Tertullian's 'crowded and twisted figures of speech' (*densis coloribus contortis*), and this very remark may serve to throw some light on Milton's opinion of the prose style of certain Fathers.

In *Of Reformation* Milton is anything but gentle in his handling of patristic rhetoric, for he says:

But let the scriptures be hard; are they more hard, more crabbed, more abstruse than the fathers? He that cannot understand the sober, plain, and unaffected style of the scriptures, will be ten times more puzzled with the knotty Africanisms, the pampered metaphors, the intricate and involved sentences of the fathers, besides the fantastic and declamatory flashes, the cross-jingling periods which cannot but disturb, and come thwart a settled devotion, worse than the din of bells and rattles.[53]

This might seem to be a sweeping denunciation of a number of Fathers, inasmuch as Minucius Felix, Tertullian, Cyprian, Arnobius, and Lactantius were all, at one time or another, of the province of Africa. The question is whether Milton would have considered all these Fathers equally guilty of bad writing. We know that Arnobius had come under his displeasure from the *Apology for Smectymnuus*, where he refers to the 'clerks of the university' as preferring 'the gay rankness of Apuleius, Arnobius, or any modern fustianist, before the native Latinisms of Cicero.' [54] The remaining four Fathers divide quite naturally into two groups, since Cyprian followed the tradition of Tertullian, and Lactantius that of Minucius Felix. A comparison of the styles of Tertullian and Lactantius, who are the more important in their respective groups, may help to establish just what Fathers Milton had in mind when he made his denunciation.

The accepted epithet for Lactantius, 'the Christian Cicero,' is, of course, a testimony to his fluent and perspicuous prose style, and no man who had won this title by following so closely 'the native

Latinisms of Cicero' could have fallen under the condemnation of Milton on this point. Milton, rather, being himself a Latin stylist of no mean rank, must have been grateful for the smoothness and ease of Lactantius after the 'crowded and twisted figures of speech' that he found distasteful in Tertullian. A glance at the passage in Tertullian that called forth this remark [55] shows a thicket of exclamation points, which bear witness that Milton might well have been thinking of him when he spoke of 'fantastic and declamatory flashes.' Insufficient knowledge of Tertullian makes it impossible to pass a first-hand judgment on his style in this discussion, but there is an extensive study of the styles of Lactantius and Tertullian, made by Professor René Pichon. He finds Lactantius the exemplar of the classic tradition, as the follower of Cicero, while Tertullian has not the classic but a purely personal style. Some of Professor Pichon's observations on Tertullian sound like elaborations of Milton's own remarks on the Fathers in general. Instead of 'cross-jingling periods,' the French investigator speaks of

consonances entre membres de phrases consécutifs; . . . une sorte de prose rimée curieuse, capable parfois de

donner du relief aux rapprochements ou oppositions
d'idées, mais monotone et fatigante à force d'être fac-
tice. . . . Il s'amuse à de vains cliquetis de mots qu'il
entre-choque et heurte sans que la pensée l'exige, à des
concetti antithétiques, parfois même à des assonances
puériles, à de véritables calembours.[56]

Where Milton censures 'fantastic and declamatory
flashes,' Professor Pichon says of Tertullian, 'Sa
passion éclate en cris imprévus, se dégageant par
une brusque explosion de la rhétorique raffinée qui
l'enveloppe, créant des exclamations haletantes,
des apostrophes, des répliques brutales comme des
coups de massue.'[57]   From the accusation of 'pampered metaphors,' however, Tertullian must be ab-
solved, since Professor Pichon says that he had
little taste for excessive, or, indeed, for many metaphors, being too oratorically minded to indulge in
that kind of figure of speech. As to the Lactantian
style, Professor Pichon again and again emphasizes
its essentially classic nature, 'absolument, exclu-
sivement classique.'[58]   He finds in this respect a
marked difference between Lactantius and the rest
of the African Fathers, except, of course, Minucius
Felix,[59] a difference so marked, indeed, that Professor Pichon claims Lactantius as one of the best

examples to disprove the theory of the influence of
race and climate on literature. In view, then, of
this analysis, it seems indubitable that it was not
'the Christian Cicero' whom Milton had in mind
when he was disparaging patristic style, but such
writers as Arnobius, Tertullian, and, to a less extent, his follower, Cyprian.

Lactantius' attack on the drama, mentioned in
the *Commonplace Book*,[60] is intimately connected
with his theory of the essential unworthiness of the
senses as such. He held that, unless the senses are
made to serve God, as in the singing and hearing
of His praises, they are snares of death.[61] Spectacles, which include both gladiatorial shows and the
drama itself, are condemned as belonging to the
pleasures of the eyes, and the subject-matter of
tragedies as well as of comedies is declared dis-
graceful and indecent. This wholesale condemnation of the stage would have been agreeable to
many Puritans, but Milton did not share their
sentiments. 'Remove the corruptions of the thea-
tre,' is the gist of his comment on Lactantius and
Tertullian in the *Commonplace Book*, 'but it would
be absurd to do away with all things dramatic.
For what is more sacred or more exalted than true

tragedy?' The note ends with the remark that
Lactantius would also take away music from
Christians.[62] There is no comment on this statement; apparently Milton felt that such a proposi-
tion was its own comment. For this attack on the
drama by one patristic authority, Milton finds a
balance in the approval of another, for he says, in
the foreword to *Samson Agonistes*, 'Gregory Nazianzen, a Father of the Church, thought it not un-
beseeming the sancity of his person to write a
tragedy, which he entitled *Christ Suffering*.' [63]

Thus, in the *Commonplace Book*, we find Milton
noting from Lactantius a surprising variety of
opinions and ideas, for at his instigation Milton
was considering the vigor of true righteousness, the
defence of the man who will not avenge himself,
the sin of sodomy, the fact that man's peculiar
strength lies in his reasoning faculty, the possibility
that patriotism may be carried too far, and the corruptions of the stage. There is, of course, no cri-
terion to determine the instances, if any, where
Lactantius started Milton to thinking along these
lines; the chances would seem to be that the
Latin Father, who was not a great, original thinker,
was rather presenting interesting considerations

on points which had already engaged Milton's thoughts. However that may be, the variety of the notes shows that Milton was reading his Lactantius thoughtfully and carefully, and was stopping by the way to ponder him.

III

LACTANTIUS IN THE "COMMENTARIES"

THE names of Lactantius and Milton have not often been coupled. Except for a few hints thrown out by the voluminous eighteenth-century commentators, it has remained for recent articles to call attention to the possibility of such an influence. Preoccupation with the influence of the classics is probably the reason why so few editors have dealt with the connection between Milton and the Church Fathers. But even of those who have realized that there was a relationship between the Fathers of the Church and the author of *Paradise Lost*, there have been few to mention so much as the name of Lactantius. Since the days of seventeenth-century ecclesiastical debate, the Fathers have declined in literary and historical prestige, and Lactantius has been, quite undeservedly, one of the least known of that reverend group.

If one goes back to Milton's earliest commentator, Patrick Hume, who masqueraded under the

title 'P. H. Φιλοποιήτης,' one finds that the
patristic tradition in scholarship was still alive in
1695. Hume shows his familiarity with many of
the Fathers and quotes them, but a somewhat
cursory search through his 'Annotations' [1] fails to
discover the name of Lactantius. The range of
P. H.'s choice in patristic quotation is shown by
the fact that, in the notes on the first book alone
of *Paradise Lost*, he quotes Augustine,[2] Jerome,[3]
Tertullian,[4] Chrysostom,[5] Basil,[6] and Theodoret,[7]
while he also makes mention of Ambrose,[8] Origen,[9]
and Athanasius,[10] without quotation.

If one may judge from the lack of attention
paid to one of Hume's notes, his 'Annotations' must
have remained unread by many a commentator.
The note is on the lines (*Paradise Lost*, i, 510–512):

> Titan, Heaven's first-born,
> With his enormous brood, and birthright seized
> By younger Saturn.

These lines have proved a source of puzzle and
even of downright error to a surprising number of
editors of Milton. The Hesiodic genealogy makes
the Titans, not a single Titan, the offspring of
Heaven and Earth, and gives them individual
names.[11] With the collective term 'the Titans'

in mind, several editors have had the temerity to attack Milton's knowledge of mythology, never having heard themselves of the single individual named Titan.[12] Had these puzzled editors but consulted the first of their line of commentators on Milton, they would have found an explanation of the passage, which would have settled all their difficulties, for Hume gives an excellent summary of the legend of the quarrel between Titan and Saturn.

Who, then, was Milton's informant on this point? Probably Lactantius, who gives an account, from Ennius' translation of Euhemerus, of the strife between Titan and his younger brother, Saturn, a story which does not tally with Hesiod's.[13] According to the bare outline of the account, Titan, being personally inferior to Saturn, yielded him the kingdom, on condition that if Saturn had any sons, they should not be allowed to grow up. After the slaying of the first son, Saturn's wife, Ops, bore twins, Jupiter and Juno, but allowed Saturn no knowledge of Jupiter. Neptune and Pluto were concealed in the same manner. Titan, on learning of the deception, with his sons, the Titans, seized Saturn and Ops, who were later set free by their son, Jupiter. Strife then followed between Jupiter and Saturn, which ended in Saturn's banishment and Jupiter's seizure of his kingdom.

If, for the sake of hypothesis, we suppose that Milton did not get his original information on Titan directly from Lactantius, there are still channels through which the Lactantian story could have reached him, namely, Boccaccio's *Genealogiae Deorum* [14] and Caxton's *Recuyell of the Historyes of Troye*. I am indebted to Professor J. S. P. Tatlock for the information that Caxton dealt with Titan.[15] Boccaccio explicitly names Lactantius as his authority,[16] and Caxton in his turn cites Boccaccio.[17] Milton would thus have been directed back, whether by one step or two, to the source of the story, even if he were reading as far afield as Caxton, and such was Milton's scholarly thoroughness that one can hardly suppose that he would have rested content with second-hand treatments of the myth when he knew its original.

To return to Lactantius in the commentators, we find no mention of the Fathers in Bentley's edition of *Paradise Lost* in 1732, or in the Richardsons' *Explanatory Notes and Remarks on Mil-*

ton's 'Paradise Lost' in 1734. Bentley, of course, must have known the Fathers with his own abounding thoroughness; he drew upon them for purposes of illustration and citation, from the time of the youthful 'Letter to Mill,' of 1691,[18] to the *Proposals for Printing a New Edition of the Greek Testament,* of 1720.[19] In his proposed edition of the New Testament, he intended to use the different readings from the Fathers of the first five centuries in the comparison of ancient versions of the New Testament, a purpose which he carried out as far as he succeeded in progressing in this labor.[20] The *Dissertation upon the Epistles of Phalaris* also makes use of the Fathers, in mentioning Lactantius [21] and quoting Clement of Alexandria.[22] But, with all his wealth of patristic learning, Bentley never applied it to the illumination of the text of *Paradise Lost,* and one can only conjecture that it never occurred to him to do so, in his zeal to right the wrongs done to Milton by his careless amanuensis and his conscienceless editor.

The first commentator to draw on Lactantius for passages parallel to Milton was John Callander of Craigforth, whose notes appeared in the Glasgow edition of 1750 of the first book of *Paradise Lost*. Lactantius is only one of several Fathers whom he cites; the list comprises Augustine,[23] Jerome,[24] Arnobius,[25] Origen,[26] Justin Martyr,[27] Clement of Alexandria,[28] and Eusebius.[29] These patristic citations show the learning and thoroughness of Callander's notes, which furnish a happy hunting-ground for the student of research, but which render this edition of the poem unwieldy and cumbersome for the less specialized reader.

An example of Callander's style is the note on the sacrifice of children to Moloch, *Paradise Lost*, i, 395.[30] Here he mentions Lactantius as accusing the Cyprians, Scythians, Gauls, and Latins of all being guilty of the crime of child-sacrifice. But Callander is not so much looking for the source of Milton's knowledge of this practice as he is seeking illustrations of it from his reading, and the result is a lengthy note, giving examples of the sacrifice of children from the works of Philo Byblius, Plato, Eusebius, Lactantius, Aelian, Euripides, Tacitus, Ennius, Varro, Saxo Grammaticus, and Olaus Magnus, named in that order. There are accounts of the same grisly rite in two seventeenth-century travel books, Sandys' *Travailes* [31] and *Purchas his*

Pilgrimage.[32] These repetitions of the Moloch story might not have appealed to Callander as being classical enough to name in his list, yet they contain details, such as the use of the word 'timbrels' in line 894, that are very close to Milton.

The next appearance of Lactantius in Callander's edition is in a note on the nature of angels, *Paradise Lost*, i, 429,[33] where the words 'bright or obscure' are explained by the idea that the devil can at will assume the shape of an angel of light, 'agreeably to what the Apostle says.'[34] Lactantius is cited as showing the power of the fallen angels to assume human shape and perform superhuman actions.

To this purpose Lactantius:

Daemones venerantur quasi terrestres Deos, et quasi depulsores malorum — qui quoniam sunt spiritus tenues, et incomprehensibiles, insinuant se corporibus hominum, et occulte in visceribus operati valetudinem vitiant, morbos citant, somniis animos terrent, mentes furoribus quatiunt.[35]

And again:

Hi spiritus contaminati, ac perditi, per omnem terram vagantur, et solatium perditionis suae perdendis hominibus operantur. Itaque omnia insidiis, fraudibus, dolis, erroribus complent. Adhaerent enim singulis hominibus, et ostiatim omnes domos occupant.[36]

To illustrate still further this subject of angels and
daemons, Callander marshals an array of references
from Socrates, Menander, Horace, Hesiod, the
Book of Daniel, and Prudentius, with no hint that
one rather than another of these classic authorities
may have influenced Milton.

Again Callander quotes Lactantius in considering the lines (*Paradise Lost*, i, 482–484) where
Milton blames the Israelites' fashioning of the gol-
den calf on Egyptian example.[37] Callander mentions Jerome first, with only a reference in a sub-
footnote to the number of the chapter where the
Father records this idea.[38] But Lactantius, who
is quoted in the text of the note, seems to have
appealed to Callander as the more important of
the authorities on this particular point:

> Some of the ancient commentators were of this senti-
> ment, as Jerome . . . and Lactantius, who when speak-
> ing of the coming of the Jews out of Egypt, 'Depulsa
> jam servitute — in luxuriam prolapsi, ad prophanos
> Egyptiorum ritus animos transtulerunt — aureum caput
> bovis, quem vocant Apim, — quod eos in signum prae-
> cederet, figurarunt.' [39]

Callander goes further than in either of the previous notes toward considering Lactantius as an
actual source of *Paradise Lost*, when he says, 'Mil-

ton here seems to follow their opinion who suppose
that Aaron took the form of a calf, and paid divine
honours to it, from what he had seen practised
among the Egyptians with regard to their Apis.'
Of the two 'ancient commentators' whom Callander adduces as being of this opinion, he seems to
consider Lactantius the more explicit and significant. This note by the Scotch commentator accordingly appears to be the first in which Lactantius figures as a possible source for Milton, rather
than as a mere provider of illustrative material.

There is another possible link between Lactantius and Milton in the lines on the genealogy of
the Olympian gods (*Paradise Lost*, i, 508–510):

> The Ionian gods — of Javan's issue held
> Gods, yet confessed later than Heaven and Earth,
> Their boasted parents.

This idea of the priority of heaven and earth over
the earliest gods is part of the argument against
the Greek deities in the first book of Lactantius,
who had for his thesis, 'The gods of the pagans
were deified mortals: therefore their worship is
false.' Callander notes one of his passages,[40] after
quoting 'Orpheus,' Homer, Hesiod, and Aeschylus on Saturn's parentage: 'To the same purpose

Lactantius, "Non poterat enim dicere (Orpheus) Jovem esse principem rerum, qui erat Saturno genitus, neque Saturnum ipsum qui Coelo natus ferebatur."' [41] Callander's next statement, that 'in the first ages it was common to say of a person whose origin and birth was unknown, that he was the son of Heaven and Earth,' is in part an echo of a remark by Minucius Felix, which Lactantius quotes in the same book as Callander is citing in his note:

> Minucius Felix in eo libro qui Octauius inscribitur sic argumentatus est: Saturnum . . . Caeli filium dictum, quod soleamus eos quorum uirtutem miremur aut eos qui repentino aduenerint, de caelo cecidisse dicere, Terrae autem, quod ignotis parentibus natos terrae filios nominemus. [42]

There is another passage [43] which Callander might have cited on the origin of Saturn, for this is a favorite idea with Lactantius. The discussion of the birth of the god is part of the euhemeristic argument of Lactantius, that Saturn was not actually heaven-born, but was merely the son of a mortal named Uranus.[44] All this emphasis in Lactantius on pagan acknowledgments that Heaven and Earth, or Uranus and Gaia, antedated the gods of the Greek mythology, may well have given Milton his idea, in the passage on the Ionian gods, of the 'boasted parents.'

A few lines farther on, Callander cites Lactantius again, on the triad of brothers, Jupiter, Neptune, and Pluto: [45]

> Lactantius gives the best, and, as it would seem, the true account of the origin of this fable; [46] he supposes it to be a fragment of ancient history, importing that the empire of the then known world was divided among the three brothers, to Jupiter the Oriental part was allotted, which was called heaven, as being the region of light, or the sun, to Pluto the Occidental, or darker regions, and to Neptune the sovereignty of the seas. This agrees exactly with Homer's account. [47]

There is no place here for so much as a hint that the Lactantian material might be regarded as a source, since Callander is not explaining the text so much as he is elaborating his statement at the beginning of the note, 'Every one knows that Jupiter was the son of Saturn and Rhea.'

Lactantius appears again in Callander's comment on the line, 'So Jove usurping reigned' (*Paradise Lost*, i, 514): [48]

> Lactantius expresses himself much in the same manner, when speaking of this action of Jupiter's, 'Nonne

a prima sua pueritia impius ac paene parricida depre-
henditur? Cum patrem regno expulit ac fugavit. Nec
expectavit mortem decrepiti senis cupiditate regnandi.'[49]

The burial of Jove in Crete, cited by Lactantius
from Ennius' translation of Euhemerus,[50] is the
subject of another note on the same line: [51] 'Lactantius cites two verses from the Sybil to the same
purpose,

Δαίμονας ἀψύχους νεκυῶν εἴδωλα καμόντων
Ὧν (sic) Κρήτη καύχημα τάφους ἡ δύσμορος ἴσχε.'

The last occurrence of Lactantius in Callander's
notes is without quotation. The editor is discussing the angels' foreknowledge that man was to be
created, in *Paradise Lost*, i, 649–654, and says, 'It
seems not improbable that Milton took this hint
from the Jewish traditions, which says that God
consulted the angels about the creation of man.' [52]
A few sentences farther on Callander remarks,

It is an opinion which has been pretty much entertained by some of the ancient Christians, as Irenaeus,
Lactantius, etc., that the angels being informed of God's
intention to create man after his own image, and to
dignify human nature by Christ's assuming it, some of
them thinking their glory hereby eclipsed, envied man's
happiness, and so revolted.

There is no reference given for Lactantius, and, after a thorough search of his works, I fail to identify the passage. May not Callander have been confused in his reference? His failure to cite book and chapter, according to his custom, makes one suspect this, and also the intricacy of the subject is sufficient to lead even the wary astray.

The question of the fall of the angels is a knotty one, which Professor Saurat has traced from Genesis to Augustine in his *La pensée de Milton*.[53] According to his outline of the question, there are two traditions of the fall of the angels. The first, springing from the sixth chapter of Genesis, makes it occur long after the fall of man, and gives sensuality as its cause, in the union of the 'sons of God' with the daughters of men. This story is followed by the apocryphal *Book of Enoch*, in the fragment of Syncellus, — of which more hereafter, —[54] and is repeated by certain of the Fathers, among whom is Lactantius.[55] The Christian tradition, that the fall of Satan, as distinguished from that of the other angels, was due to envy of the Son of God and preceded the fall of man, is handed down by such Fathers as Justin, Athenagoras, Irenaeus, Cyprian,[56] and Lactantius, to be given final form by Augustine. The confusion of the various traditions among the early Fathers is exemplified in the works of Lactantius, who attributes to Satan envy of both Christ and Adam, and also repeats the story of the angels' sin with women.[57]

In the eighth chapter of the second book of the *Divine Institutes*, Lactantius gives his decidedly Arian version of the creation of the Son by the Father, the subsequent creation of 'another being, in whom the disposition of the divine origin did not remain,'[58] and the envy entertained by this second spirit for the Son, an envy which is declared to be the source of all evils.[59] Again, in the twelfth chapter of the same book [60] and in the *Epitome*,[61] it is envy of Adam that, Lactantius implies, is at the root of all the woes and evils that beset mankind. Although Professor Saurat fails to make one point clear, that Satan's initial envy of Christ and the serpent's subsequent envy of Adam occur in the accounts of two quite separate events, the former in the fall of Satan, the latter in that of man, yet the French critic seems to be quite correct in his main contention, of the 'incoherence of the traditions' in general.

Since, then, in the works of this one Father we find interwoven the different strands of Judaic and Christian legends, it seems not at all impossible that Callander may have made a mistake in following out one strand of the web, and have wrongly attributed to Lactantius the idea of the angels' jealousy of man before his creation. At any rate, this single slip would hardly invalidate the worth of Callander's observation of some of the links between Lactantius and Milton, which he seems to have been the first to record.

There is a curious point in Miltonic scholarship which Callander's wide reading enabled him to be the first to explain, the meaning of the name 'Azazel' for Satan's standard-bearer in *Paradise Lost*, i, 533-534,

> That proud honour claimed
> Azazel as his right, a Cherub tall.[62]

Here, again, there are modern commentators who would have profited by reading an earlier note. Verity, for instance, quite evidently had never read Callander on this subject, but went on hunting for the source.[63] The neglect of the contributions made by such an editor as Callander would

furnish an excellent text for a sermon on the use
of earlier commentators by the later.

Close on the heels of Callander's work came
Bishop Newton's edition of *Paradise Regained*,
published in 1752, which draws on Lactantius for
occasional citations. Newton himself is not the
author of these particular notes, with one possible
exception, which will be discussed later.[64] That
Newton knew Lactantius is clear, however, from
the number of times he cites the Father in the
Dissertations on the Prophecies,[65] but it is from his
correspondent, the Reverend Mr. Calton,[66] that he
derives the notes on Lactantius.

Calton does not quote as many Fathers as does
Callander, but confines himself to Augustine,[67]
Athanasius,[68] and Justin Martyr,[69] besides Lactantius. In spite of belonging to the school of
Bentley, Calton was not carried to such lengths
by the joy of emendation. In *Paradise Regained*,
ii, 60, for example, he would like to believe that,
in place of 'But to his mother Mary,' Milton
dictated 'But O! his mother Mary,' a change on
which he remarks,[70] 'See the happy effect of a very
small alteration! The transition to the great
mother is freed from an aukward (sic) elleipsis;

and the poet brings her upon the scene with a compassionate feeling of her grief.' This satisfaction with his emendation is a little like the complacency of Addison's Ned Softly over the 'But ah!' in his verses.

There are only three notes in all on Lactantian parallels by Calton, two in *Paradise Regained* and one in *Samson Agonistes*. The first applies to *Paradise Regained*, i, 163–167:

> That all the Angels and ethereal Powers —
> They now, and men hereafter — may discern
> From what consummate virtue I have chose
> This perfect man, by merit called my Son,
> To earn salvation for the sons of men.

The note, dealing with the nature of Christ, begins, 'Not a word is said here of the Son of God, but what a Socinian would allow. His divine nature is artfully concealed under a partial and ambiguous representation.'[71] Calton goes on to quote Justin Martyr, to the effect that 'Christ, considered only as man, deserved for his superior wisdom to be called the Son of God.' Again he says that the words 'consummate virtue,' being referable to either the human or the divine nature of Christ, are ambiguous. The use of this word 'virtue' he illustrates by a quotation from the *Divine Institutes*.[72] It is noteworthy that Calton uses the words of Justin Martyr and of Lactantius as illustrating his own point, rather than as sources of Milton's thought.

Newton again quotes Calton on *Paradise Regained*, i, 453, with reference to Satan's presiding over oracles. The note reads:

The Demons (Lactantius says) could certainly foresee, and truly foretell many future events, from the knowledge they had of the dispositions of Providence before their fall. And then they assumed all the honor to themselves, pretending to be the authors, and doers of what they predicted. Nam cum dispositiones Dei praesentiant, quippe qui ministri ejus fuerunt, interponunt se in his rebus; ut quaecunque à Deo vel facta sunt, vel fiunt, ipsi potissimum facere, aut fecisse videantur. Div. Inst. ii, 16.[73]

Another sentence from the same chapter is quoted by Professor A. S. Cook in his *Notes on Milton's Nativity Ode:* [74] 'They [daemons] especially deceive in the case of oracles, the juggleries of which the profane cannot distinguish from the truth.' [75] Thus Lactantius is added to the list of authors, beginning with Plutarch in the *De Defectu Oraculorum*,[76] from whom Milton may have drawn his knowledge of oracles.

The last passage from Lactantius in Newton's edition[77] refers to the phoenix, in *Samson Agonistes*, 1705–1706:

> And, though her body dies, her fame survives,
> A secular bird, ages of lives.

The term 'secular bird' is explained by a passage from Lactantius. 'The phoenix', says he (Calton), 'liv'd *a thousand years* according to some . . . and hence it is called here *a secular bird*. Ergo quoniam sex diebus cuncta Dei opera perfecta sunt; per *secula sex* [italics Calton's], id est annorum *sex millia*, manere hoc statu mundum necesse est. Lactantius, Div. Inst. Lib. 7, c. 14.'[78] The note has not Calton's name at the end, but this part of it appears to be his, from the previous use of his name. Since, however, Newton goes on to a remark, apparently of his own, on the position of a comma, there is a possibility that the citation from Lactantius should also be attributed to the editor himself. To be sure, Newton was familiar with these particular words, having quoted them in his *Dissertations on the Prophecies*.[79]

To Calton, then, is due the credit of having been among the first to record parallels between Lactantius and Milton. The handling of these passages, however, does not lead one to think of the *Divine Institutes* as a source of *Paradise Regained*, but rather as a means of shedding light upon difficult points in the text.

After Callander and Bishop Newton, few commentators pay attention to Lactantius or to the Fathers in general, for the day of patristic popularity is over. Calton's notes, as given by Newton, are quoted by Todd[80] and Sir Egerton Brydges,[81] but, as has been said, Callander's notes seem to have been generally neglected. I fail to find any further mention of Lactantius until Masson's edition, and that note, bringing in the name of the Church Father erroneously, is hardly to Masson's credit in scholarship.

The reference in question is to Milton's lines, *Paradise Lost*, ii, 964–965,

> . . . the dreaded name
> Of Demogorgon.

Masson's note reads, 'This last awful personage, it is said, is first distinctly named in the Christian writer, Lactantius, who lived in the beginning of the fourth century. But in so naming him, Lactantius is believed to have broken the spell of a great mystery. For, though never named by the

ancients, he was known to them.' [82] The editor's
'it is said' betrays him: he is taking Lactantius on
hearsay, and behold, he has taken the wrong Lactantius! Masson should be citing, not the Christian
Father, but Lactantius Placidus, the fifth-century
scholiast of Statius.[83] This mistake is repeated by
Verity, who simply echoes Masson.[84]

The only other note on this line that Masson
uses is that by Bentley, which, curiously enough,
falls into as deep an error as Masson's own. The
person of all others one might have chosen to explain 'Demogorgon' would be Richard Bentley,
and yet he thinks that this is one of those 'barbarous names' not to be mixed with 'those of
antiquity,' supposes that Boccaccio invented the
word, and rejects the line.[85] If, however, when
Bentley failed him, Professor Masson had consulted Jortin's notes, which are given by Bishop
Newton in his edition, he would have found which
Lactantius first used the name of Demogorgon and
where. Newton says on this point, 'And besides
these authorities to justify our author, let me
farther add what the learned Mr. Jortin hath sug-
gested, that this name "is to be found in Lactantius, the Scholiast of Statius, on Thebaid. IV, 516.

Dicit Deum Demogorgona summum. . . ."''[86] All Jortin's work on this line is wasted, as far as Masson and Verity are concerned, and they themselves are guilty of an avoidable error, because of their failure to consult their own predecessor.

The last mention of Lactantius that I have succeeded in finding in a commentator is a passing reference in H. B. Sprague's note on Titan in a school edition of 1898, where, as has been pointed out,[87] the editor insists that Titan is only another name for Oceanus, the eldest of the twelve Titans.

With the exception of Callander and Calton, then, the commentators have plainly not concerned themselves with Lactantius, and it remained for Mr. A. F. Leach to call attention to such an influence in his article, 'Milton as Schoolboy and Schoolmaster,' read before the British Academy, December 10, 1908.[88] Lactantius is only one of a group of Christian authors that were prescribed for reading in St. Paul's School by John Colet in his *Statutes*,[89] and Mr. Leach contends that these authors were still read in Milton's day, and that among them Lactantius and Prudentius had a noteworthy influence on the youthful mind of Milton, which revealed itself in his later works.

Professor Masson had rather contemptuously dismissed the possibility that such a curriculum survived until Milton's time, saying, 'Instead of peddling over Sedulius and other such small practitioners of later or middle-age Latinity, recommended as proper class-books by Colet, the scholars of St. Paul's, as of other contemporary schools, were now led through very much the same list of Roman prose-writers and poets as are still honoured in our academies.' [90] But Masson does not give any authority for this statement, nor is his tone that of one who has gone deeply into the subject.

The points of likeness between Lactantius and Milton which Mr. Leach mentions are the kindred view of the position of Christ, the discouragement of the tendency to pry too far into the secrets of God, and the mention of Hermes Trismegistus, points which must all be considered later.[91] Mr. Leach strengthens his case by pointing out a number of likenesses to Prudentius in the work of Milton, and Professor Cook has done the same for Milton and Mantuanus,[92] another of Colet's ill-assorted group of Latin authors. It is the contention of this discussion that Mr. Leach is correct in his belief, that young Milton did know Lactantius, although no actual evidence of his acquaintance with the Latin Father from the days at St. Paul's has been unearthed, as had been hoped. Other data have been found, however, which go to show that the daily routine of Milton's life at school left its marks on his work.[93]

IV

OTHER EVIDENCES OF LACTANTIUS' INFLUENCE IN THE WORKS OF MILTON

THERE are two citations of Lactantius by name in Milton's prose, one in *Of Reformation*, in 1641, and one in *Tetrachordon*, in 1645. These dates help to confirm Professor Hanford's classification of the Lactantius entries as coming early in the years between 1639 and 1652.[1] This classification is based on the fact that these entries appear, from their use of the Italic 'e' and from their position, to be among the first made in the *Commonplace Book*, after the Italian journey.

The mention of Lactantius in *Of Reformation* identifies him briefly and quotes two passages from him on the theme of undue respect for ancestral opinion:

Next Lactantius, he that was preferred to have the bringing up of Constantine's children, in his second book of Institutions, chap. 7 and 8, disputes against

the vain trust in antiquity, as being the chiefest argument of the heathen against the Christians: 'They do
not consider,' saith he, 'what religion is, but they are
confident it is true, because the ancients delivered it;
they count it a trespass to examine it.' And in the
eighth: 'Not because they went before us in time, therefore in wisdom; which being given alike to all ages,
cannot be prepossessed by the ancients: wherefore, see-
ing that to seek the truth is inbred to all, they bereave
themselves of wisdom, the gift of God, who without
judgment follow the ancients, and are led by others like
brute beasts.' [2]

A secondary source from which Milton may
possibly have derived the information that Lactantius acted as tutor to Constantine's son is Carlo
Sigonio's *De Occidentali Imperio*.[3] Dr. Hale draws
attention to this parallel [4] and to Gibbon's mention of the same detail;[5] he might have strength-
ened the case for Milton's having used Sigonio by
pointing out a quotation, dealing with Constantine's reply to the Donatists, which is to be found
in the *Commonplace Book*,[6] and which is drawn
from the same third book of the *De Occidentali
Imperio* as mentions Lactantius.[7] The two passages in Sigonio are separated by only five pages
in the edition of 1593, which Milton's citations in
the *Commonplace Book* show him to have used.

Milton's quotation from Lactantius in *Of Reformation* is preceded by one from Cyprian, and just prior to that is a statement that might mislead the reader into thinking that Milton had an unfavorable opinion of both Cyprian and Lactantius. 'I must,' the poet says, 'of necessity begin from the second rank of fathers, because till then antiquity had no plea.' [8] This does not mean that he considered Lactantius as second rate, but that, as Dr. Hale paraphrases the passage, 'he will not begin with the earliest Fathers, for in their case there was no "antiquity" to refer to. By the time of Cyprian, Athanasius, Basil, etc., however, a tradition based on antiquity had grown up.' [9] Instead, apparently, of considering Lactantius inferior to the other Fathers, Milton to the contrary treats him with a consistent respect that he accords to but few of them.

The quotation from *Tetrachordon* shows Milton striving desperately to prove that the Church Father was on his side on the divorce question, while the plain facts of the case are that Lactantius would doubtless have repudiated any such position. Milton says:

Lactantius, of the age that succeeded, speaking of this matter in the 6th of his 'Institutions,' hath these words: 'But lest any think he may circumscribe divine precepts, let this be added, that all misinterpreting, and occasion of fraud or death may be removed, he commits adultery who marries the divorced wife; and besides the crime of adultery, divorces a wife that he may marry another.' To divorce and marry another, and to divorce that he may marry another, are two different things; and imply that Lactantius thought not this place the forbidding of all necessary divorce, but such only as proceeded from the wanton desire of a future choice, not from the burden of a present affliction.[10]

There is undoubtedly a legal distinction between divorcing and marrying again, and divorcing to marry again, but there is nothing to show that Lactantius was concerning himself with any such distinction. Milton seems to be reading into Lactantius the acceptance of the idea that divorce can be necessary, and the unsuccessfulness of the attempt is only too apparent. It is interesting to note that Lactantius is the only one of the Fathers quoted who required wresting from his sense in order to support Milton. Furthermore, here is Milton, who is generally supposed not to have had any use for the Fathers, producing Justin Martyr, Tertullian, Origen, Lactantius, Basil, Epiphanius,

Ambrose, Jerome, and Augustine as authorities for his side.[11] The quotation in *Tetrachordon*, which is taken from the same chapter as furnished the *Commonplace Book* with its passage on sodomy, is not an example of the repetition by Milton of an extended or important argument from Lactantius, since the Church Father has but one passing mention of divorce in his discussion of relations between the sexes. This drawing on Lactantius for confirmation is rather an example of Milton's keenness in noting or recalling even trivial details that might serve his cause.

He does not seem to have drawn on Lactantius in the rest of his prose even for unspecified hints, except in the passage from the *Areopagitica*, already mentioned, and perhaps in the view of Christ expressed in *Of Christian Doctrine*, which will be discussed in connection with *Paradise Lost*.[12]

In the poetry, however, the case is different, for there are several instances of the apparent influence of Lactantius, especially in *Paradise Lost*. A certain amount of caution is necessary when one comes to deal with the Latin Father as a source, because he is a compendium of other

men's thoughts rather than an outstanding, original thinker on his own account. The question is
often one of sheer emphasis: a given idea may be
repeated so many times by Lactantius that no
reader of his works can fail to associate it with his
name, and yet the idea came to him from some
other philosopher or poet.

This is true of the use by both Lactantius and
Milton of the argument that man's upright posture
raised him, mentally and morally, from the level
of the other animals, and exalted him to the contemplation of heaven and the worship of God.
Milton says in *Paradise Lost*, vii, 505–516:

> There wanted yet the master-work, the end
> Of all yet done — a creature who, not prone
> And brute as other creatures, but endued
> With sanctity of reason, might erect
> His stature, and upright with front serene
> Govern the rest, self-knowing, and from thence
> Magnanimous to correspond with Heaven,
> But grateful to acknowledge whence his good
> Descends; thither with heart, and voice, and eyes
> Directed in devotion, to adore
> And worship God Supreme, who made him chief
> Of all his works.

So many times does Lactantius utter this thought
that there are too many instances to quote,[13] but

the first occurrence of the argument may be taken as typical:

parens enim noster ille unus et solus cum fingeret hominem id est animal intelligens et rationis capax, eum uero ex humo subleuatum ad contemplationem sui artificis erexit. quod optime ingeniosus poeta signauit:

> pronaque cum spectent animalia cetera terram,
> os homini sublime dedit caelumque uidere
> iussit et erectos ad sidera tollere uultus.

hinc utique ἄνθρωπον Graeci appellauerunt, quod sursum spectet. ipsi ergo sibi renuntiant seque hominum nomine abdicant qui non sursum aspiciunt, sed deorsum: nisi forte id ipsum quod recti sumus sine causa homini adtributum putant. spectare nos caelum deus uoluit utique non frustra. nam et aues et ex mutis paene omnia caelum uident, sed nobis proprie datum est caelum rigidis ac stantibus intueri, ut religionem ibi quaeramus, ut deum, cuius illa sedes est, quoniam oculis non possumus, animo contemplemur: quod profecto non facit qui aes aut lapidem, quae sunt terrena, ueneratur. est autem prauissimum, cum ratio corporis recta sit, quod est temporale, ipsum uero animum, qui sit aeternus, humilem fieri, cum figura et status nihil aliut significet nisi mentem hominis eo spectare oportere quo uultum, et animum tam rectum esse debere quam corpus, ut id cui dominari debet imitetur.[14]

Compared with this passage, Milton's handling of the theme shows several points of similarity.

Where Lactantius calls man 'animal intelligens et rationis capax,' Milton speaks of him as the master work of creation, a superior creature, 'endued With sanctity of reason,' and both make his up-right posture the basis of his reason and his instinct to worship God. The question at once arises, was Lactantius Milton's source?

There is a third factor to be taken into account, a passage from Ovid on the same subject, which Lactantius quotes in several places [15] and designates as his source in the passage just cited:

> Sanctius his animal mentisque capacius altae
> Deerat adhuc, et quod dominari in cetera posset.
> Natus homo est. cive hunc divino semine fecit
> Ille opifex rerum, mundi melioris origo,
> Sive recens tellus seductaque nuper ab alto
> Aethere cognati retinebat semina caeli.
> Quam satus Iapeto, mixtam fluvialibus undis,
> Finxit in effigiem moderantum cunctam deorum.
> Pronaque cum spectent animalia cetera terram,
> Os homini sublime dedit, caelumque tueri
> Iussit et erectos ad sidera tollere vultus.
> Sic, modo quae fuerat rudis et sine imagine, tellus
> Induit ignotas hominum conversa figuras.[16]

The commentators, beginning with Hume,[17] have taken Ovid as the basis of the lines in *Paradise Lost*. Since Milton knew both his Ovid and his

Lactantius, the only means of deciding from which of them the passage in *Paradise Lost* was derived is to look for a detail which occurs in Milton and one of the other two, but not in the third. There is a surprising closeness of agreement among all three as to details, but there is one that is peculiar to Milton and Lactantius. That is the idea that man's erect stature, in enabling him to look toward heaven, calls for the worship of God in return. That is Lactantius' characteristically Christian embellishment of the thought he found in Ovid, and as such Milton seems to have taken it over. Not that the English poet did not probably remember that Ovid gave expression to the same general thought, but Milton, once having read Lactantius, could not have forgotten the number of places where he hammers away at this theme, with its Christian addition. Both Lactantius and Milton make the service of God the climax of their respective passages, and on their agreement on this particular, and on the fact that Lactantius states this form of his argument no less than ten times is based the claim that the *Divine Institutes*, rather than the *Metamorphoses*, were the basis for the version in *Paradise Lost*.

There is, to be sure, another author who makes use of the same argument for the dignity of man, Minucius Felix in the *Octavius*.[18]   He, however, employs this reasoning only once, and then without emphasis on its Christian implications.

How early, then, did Milton know the Fathers in general? There is no evidence in his schoolboy paraphrases of the Psalms that he had made their acquaintance as early as the days at St. Paul's, but, because of the obvious limitations of paraphrasing, this is no place to look for such evidence. The first mention of the Fathers is in the *Fourth Elegy*, that addressed to Thomas Young and written at Cambridge in 1627. Here Milton wonders under what circumstances his epistle will come upon his tutor, whether it will find him sitting with his wife and children, or perhaps reading the ponderous volumes of the Fathers, or the Bible itself:

> Forsitan aut veterum praelarga volumina Patrum
>   Versantem, aut veri Biblia sacra Dei.[19]

Is it mere fancy that one catches here a note of the almost inevitable weariness that comes over one who has himself pored over the 'praelarga volumina Patrum'?

The early poem that best bears out Mr. Leach's claim that Milton read Colet's Christian authors at school is the *Nativity Ode*, which, according to Professor Cook, has many similarities to the *Hymns* and the *Apotheosis* of Prudentius,[20] and to the *Bucolics* of Baptista Mantuanus.[21] Mr. Leach also notes some of these same resemblances; his remarks on Prudentius antedate those of Professor Cook, while those on Mantuanus come after the article by the American professor.[22] The influence of Prudentius on Milton deserves a full study by itself, but enough has already been accomplished to make it appear probable that Milton knew Prudentius amd Mantuanus at least by the time he wrote the *Nativity Ode*.

With the knowledge of two of Colet's group of authors established as early as 1629, the chances for Milton's having read these writers in school appears better than mere guesswork. There are only three possibilities to explain how Milton came to know them so early: that he read them in school, in college, or as part of his independent browsing during either of those periods. In default of a statement from Milton himself, or of indirect evidence from the text before 1629, the only clue

we have as to which of these three possibilities was
true, is the one assured fact that Colet, in 1518,
had prescribed the reading of these same authors
by St. Paul's scholars. It hardly seems a rash
guess that the school would still be observing
Colet's *Statutes* only a century later. To accept
either of the other possibilities, that Milton first
met this group of authors in college work, or that
he found them out for himself, one must assume
that Colet's most clearly expressed wishes were
in one respect totally disregarded by the school
he founded, within one hundred years of its foundation. And that must be assumed of a school
famous for its respect for tradition! It would
seem less of a strain on the inherent probabilities
of the case to suppose that Colet's *Statutes* were
observed, and that Milton read Prudentius and
Mantuanus and Lactantius at St. Paul's.

Of Sedulius, the fourth of Dean Colet's group,
an Irish poet who wrote majestic Latin, Mr. Leach
says, 'It is doubtful how far Sedulius was read at
St. Paul's, his Paschal feast savouring too much of
the mass.' Dr. George Sigerson, in *The Easter Song
of Sedulius*, says nothing about Milton's having
known that writer early in his career, but believes

him to have been deeply indebted to Sedulius in
both *Paradise Lost* and *Paradise Regained*. Dr.
Sigerson attempts to evaluate this debt, but his
frankly partisan attitude toward his subject makes
it impossible to accept his evidence, although such
proof would help the case for Milton's study of
Colet's authors. *Paradise Lost*, under Dr. Sigerson's treatment, is made to appear little better
than a plagiarism of the *Carmen Paschale* of Sedulius, with no consideration of the fact that the
two poets were writing on a common theme, the
fall of man and his redemption by Christ. Neither
is any allowance made for the influence of the
Bible, which seems to explain every point of resemblance between the two poems. If Milton says
more than Sedulius, he is said to be developing
and amplifying; [23] if he says less, he is 'omitting
or abbreviating or qualifying'; [24] never is it granted
that the English poet improved on his supposed
model, the Irish one. Dr. Sigerson even claims
that the most Miltonic thing about Milton, his
style, is acquired from Sedulius,[25] and as for *Paradise Regained*, it is an acknowledged failure, because Milton tried to 'fill out the simple and
sufficient structure of Sedulius with interminable

speeches.'[26]   Dr. Sigerson does not stop to consider that the brief résumé of the life of Christ in
Sedulius had a purely narrative purpose, quite different from Milton's, which was expository, in
showing the Saviour's reconquest of the citadel of
man's integrity, in the name of man, and by the
use of reason. There is here, then, no confirmation of Milton's knowledge of Sedulius or of Mr.
Leach's theory, and we must return to Lactantius.

The earliest hint of Lactantian influence is in
Comus, and this, again, is not an undisputed case.
In his famous speech on chastity, the Elder
Brother defines the doctrine of the corporality of
the sinful soul, and says:

> But, when lust,
> By unchaste looks, loose gestures, and foul talk,
> But most by lewd and lavish act of sin,
> Lets in defilement to the inward parts,
> The soul grows clotted by contagion,
> Imbodies, and imbrutes, till she quite lose
> The divine property of her first being.[27]

This theory is shared by Lactantius, in the seventh
book of the *Divine Institutes*, where he is answering
the question how, if the soul be immortal, it can
yet feel physical pain in the after life. He says:

huic quaestioni siue argumento a Stoicis ita occurritur
. . . impias uero, quoniam se malis cupiditatibus in-
quinauerint, mediam quandam gerere inter immortalem
mortalemque naturam et habere aliquid inbecillitatis
ex contagione carnis, cuius desideriis ac libidinibus ad-
dictae ineluibilem quendam fucum trahant labemque
terrenam: quae cum temporis diurnitate penitus inhae-
serit, eius naturae reddi animas, ut si non extinguibiles
in totum, quoniam ex deo sint, tamen cruciabiles fiant
per corporis maculam, quae peccatis inusta sensum do-
loris adtribuit.[28]

Here is what looks, on the surface, like a clear
case of direct influence, for the thought is the same,
there is the identical word 'contagion,' used by
both, and Lactantius' *malis cupiditatibus* and *desideriis ac libidinibus* correspond to Milton's more
specific description of the manifestations of lust.
But Lactantius, not stopping here, goes on to quote
Virgil, showing another possible source for the idea.
The passage that the Church Father quotes is from
the sixth book of the *Aeneid*:

Quin et supremo cum lumine vita reliquit,
Non tamen omne malum miseris nec funditus omnes
Corporeae excedunt pestes, penitusque necesse est
Multa diu concreta modis inolescere miris.
Ergo exercentur poenis veterumque malorum
Supplicia expendunt.[29]

There are no links between Virgil and Milton beyond the general thought; the *Aeneid* does not even specify the sins of the erring soul as lust, and there are no words the common use of which binds the two poems together. The commentary of Servius on *Aeneid*, vi, 724, uses the word *contagiones:* 'ita ergo et animus quamdiu est in corpore, patitur eius contagiones,' as also in vi, 719: 'credendum est animas corporis contagione pollutas ad caelum reverti?' [30] But, as in the passage in Virgil, there is again no such emphasis on the lusts of the flesh in Servius' comment as a whole as there is in Lactantius.

The same idea occurs in Chaucer, in the *Second Nun's Prologue*, 71–74:

> And of thy light my soule in prison lighte,
> That troubled is by the contagioun
> Of my body, and also by the wighte
> Of erthly luste and fals affeccioun.

This resemblance, however, is too slight to be significant, inasmuch as there is here none of that consideration of the nature of the lustful soul, 'between immortal and mortal,' that both Lactantius and Milton are concerned with.

The passage one might have expected Lactantius to quote, one which he may have known and which Milton certainly knew, is that in the *Phaedo* which gave this doctrine its most famous form. Socrates says, in Jowett's translation:

But the soul which has been polluted, and is impure at the time of her departure, and is the companion and servant of the body always, and is in love with and fascinated by the body and by the desires and pleasures of the body, until she is led to believe that the truth only exists in a bodily form, which a man may touch and see and taste, and use for the purposes of his lusts, — the soul, I mean, accustomed to hate and fear and avoid the intellectual principle, which to the bodily eye is dark and invisible, and can be attained only by philosophy; — do you suppose that such a soul will depart pure and unalloyed?

That is impossible, he (*i. e.* Cebes) replied.

She is held fast by the corporeal, which the continual association and constant care of the body made natural to her.

Very true.

And this, my friend, may be conceived to be that heavy, weighty, earthy element of sight by which such a soul is depressed and dragged down again into the visible world, because she is afraid of the invisible and of the world below — prowling about tombs and sepulchres, in the neighbourhood of which, as they tell us, are seen certain ghostly apparitions of souls which have not departed pure, but are cloyed with sight and therefore visible.[31]

Milton's description of

> those thick and gloomy shadows damp
> Oft seen in charnel-vaults and sepulchres,
> Lingering and sitting by a new-made grave,[32]

leaves no doubt that he had the passage from Plato in mind when he was writing *Comus*, or else that it had sunk into the very tissue of his memory and needed not to be specifically recalled. But the presence of Plato in this passage does not necessarily argue the absence of Lactantius. Both might have been and probably were recalled, Lactantius for the 'contagion of the flesh,' and Plato for the haunting of charnel houses by the sinful soul. No one knew better than a classical scholar of Milton's stamp that Lactantius and Plato were talking about two different things as reasons for the punishment of the soul by corporality: Plato meant the tendency of the average soul to seek a physical answer to its philosophical questionings, 'to believe that truth only exists in a bodily form,' [33] while Lactantius meant nothing more than 'the sinful lusts of the flesh.' The word 'lust' to the Greek meant the hankering of the soul after some

physical embodiment of its desires, and it seems
to be Lactantius, rather than Plato, that Milton
follows in making mere fleshly lust the cause of the
embodiment of the soul after death. The fact,
then, that Milton employed the patristic, rather
than the Greek, conception of lust, and that he
apparently borrowed the word 'contagion,' are the
main factors in the evidence that he was drawing
on Lactantius as well as on Plato in writing *Comus*.
If this be allowed, then Milton's knowledge of the
Christian Father in the Horton period is established at 1634, setting forward the date by at least
five years from that of the material in the *Commonplace Book* and by seven years from the first dated
use of Lactantius in *Of Reformation*, in 1641.

There is another possible trace of Lactantius in
the early poems, a verbal resemblance in the description of fame in *Lycidas*, 81–82, where Phoebus
declares that it

> . . . lives and spreads aloft by those pure eyes
> And perfect witness of all-judging Jove.

Very similar is Lactantius' account of virtue triumphant over all adversities:

quid enim, 'si,' ut Furius dicebat, 'rapiatur uexetur
exterminetur egeat, auferantur ei manus, effodiantur

oculi, damnetur uinciatur uratur, miseris etiam modis
necetur,' perdetne suum praemium uirtus aut potius
peribit ipsa? minime, sed et mercedem suam deo iudice
accipiet et uiuet ac semper uigebit.[34]

This likeness, occurring in only a few words, may
be sheer coincidence, but the expression *deo iudice*
and the verbs *uiuet* and *uigebit* are quite close
enough to Milton to be considered as a possible
influence. It must be remembered, too, that the
'fame' of *Lycidas* has taken on a certain coloring
that makes the term very closely akin to the
'virtue' that Lactantius is describing.

The incomprehensibility of God by the finite
mind is a point that Lactantius deals with, and
that Milton considered in his turn. This thought
is not the property of the Fathers; it lies behind
the great question asked of Job, 'Where wast thou
when I laid the foundations of the earth? declare,
if thou hast understanding.'[35] In three separate
passages Milton declares the mysteries of God to
be beyond human reach. The first is in Raphael's
reply to Adam's request for knowledge of the
Creation (*Paradise Lost*, vii, 111–130):

> 'This also thy request, with caution asked,
> Obtain; though to recount almighty works
> What words or tongue of Seraph can suffice,

Or heart of man suffice to comprehend?
Yet what thou canst attain, which best may serve
To glorify the Maker, and infer
Thee also happier, shall not be withheld
Thy hearing.   Such commission from above
I have received, to answer thy desire
Of knowledge within bounds; beyond abstain
To ask, nor let thine own inventions hope
Things not revealed, which the invisible King,
Only omniscient, hath suppressed in night,
To none communicable in Earth or Heaven.
Enough is left besides to search and know;
But Knowledge is as food, and needs no less
Her temperance over appetite, to know
In measure what the mind may well contain;
Oppresses else with surfeit, and soon turns
Wisdom to folly, as nourishment to wind. . . .'

Raphael repeats his caution against prying into
the secrets of God in the next book (*Paradise Lost*,
viii, 66–75):

'To ask or search I blame thee not; for Heaven
Is as the Book of God before thee set,
Wherein to read his wondrous works, and learn
His seasons, hours, or days, or months, or years.
This to attain, whether Heaven move or Earth
Imports not, if thou reckon right; the rest
From Man or Angel the great Architect
Did wisely to conceal, and not divulge
His secrets, to be scanned by them who ought
Rather admire . . .'

And yet again, at the end of the same speech, the
Archangel warns against seeking to know what is
beyond human power of comprehension:

> 'Solicit not thy thoughts with matters hid:
> Leave them to God above; him serve and fear.
> Of other creatures as him pleases best,
> Wherever placed, let him dispose; joy thou
> In what he gives to thee, this Paradise
> And thy fair Eve; Heaven is for thee too high
> To know what passes there. Be lowly wise;
> Think only what concerns thee and thy being;
> Dream not of other worlds, what creatures there
> Live, in what state, condition, or degree —
> Contented that thus far hath been revealed
> Not of Earth only, but of highest Heaven.' [36]

Contentment with circumscribed knowledge, even
though the limitations be imposed by an angel, is
hardly a doctrine that one expects to find preached
by the author of the *Areopagitica*. This idea would
seem scarcely to have been native to him, but the
question where he got it is to be answered by a
study of patristic sources.

Lactantius has scattered through his work a
number of passages expressing the same thought:

. . . qui uocatur deus, cuius principium quoniam non
potest conprehendi, ne quaeri quidem debet. satis est
homini ad plenam perfectamque prudentiam, si deum

esse intellegat. cuius intellegentiae uis et summa haec
est, ut suspiciat et honorificet communem parentem
generis humani et rerum mirabilium fabricatorem.[37]

In another chapter of the same book, he says:

sciat igitur quam inepte faciat qui res inenarrabiles
quaerat. hoc est enim modum condicionis suae trans-
gredi nec intellegere quousque homini liceat accedere.
. . . quid ergo quaeris quae nec potes scire nec si scias,
beatior fics? perfecta est in homine sapientia, si et deum
esse unum et ab ipso facta esse uniuersa cognoscat.[38]

Mr. Leach has already noted the likeness between
this passage and the lines from the seventh book
of *Paradise Lost*, and makes the positive statement,
'Certainly Raphael's speech to Adam is indebted
to Lactantius.' [39] Other passages dealing with the
same thought, which Mr. Leach has not noted,
need not be separately cited.[40] The similarity in
thought between Milton and Lactantius is so close
that one would feel safe in declaring it, with Mr.
Leach, a reminiscence of the one by the other,
were it not for an entry in the *Commonplace Book*,
which shows that it was Eusebius, rather than
Lactantius, that Milton wanted to recall as having
expressed this idea. The *Commonplace Book* says,
under the heading, '*De Curiositate*':

Quaestiones profundas de deo quas humana ratio
difficilius interpretetur, aut assequatur, aut non cogi-
tandas, aut silentio premendas ne in vulgus edantur,
deturque hinc materies schismatum in Ecclesia, sapien-
tissime monet *Constantinus* in Epist. ad Alexandrum et
Arium. *Euseb.* in ejus vitâ, l. 2, c. 77, et apud *Socrat.*,
l. I.[41]

This entry, which is another instance of Milton's
summarizing a passage instead of quoting it, is
among the earliest made in the *Commonplace Book*,
according to the evidence of handwriting, and
shows that he was reading Eusebius before 1639.[42]
Milton merely gives the gist of Constantine's letter
to Alexander and Arius, as reported by Eusebius,[43]
while in Socrates there is no word of this letter, but
only the relation of the strife of ecclesiastical fac-
tions over Arius.[44] Although the *Commonplace
Book* shows that it was Eusebius with whom Milton originally connected the idea that God's
secrets are beyond human reach, it is safe to add
that this thought must have been further empha-
sized in his mind by the insistence of Lactantius
upon it. To say more than this would be to trespass on probability.

One idea about God that may have reached
Milton by way of Lactantius is that of His sexless-

ness. It is one that an early Christian Father did well to emphasize, in the face of the innumerable legends of the gods' amorous adventures on which his converts had been raised, but it seems curious to find Milton emphasizing this idea in the seventeenth century:

> 'Thou in thyself art perfect, and in thee
> Is no deficience found. Not so is Man,
> But in degree — the cause of his desire
> By conversation with his like to help
> Or solace his defects. No need that thou
> Shouldst propagate, already infinite,
> And through all numbers absolute, though One;
> But Man by number is to manifest
> His single imperfection, and beget
> Like of his like, his image multiplied,
> In unity defective; which requires
> Collateral love, and dearest amity.
> Thou, in thy secrecy although alone,
> Best with thyself accompanied, seek'st not
> Social communication . . .'[45]

This is but a rendering into verse of the view expressed in the severely unadorned prose of the *Of Christian Doctrine:*

Poterat enim Deus certe salva essentia sua non genuisse; cum ad essentiam Dei, qui propagatione prorsus non indiget, generatio nihil pertineat: quod autem ad

essentiam suam sive naturam nihil pertinet, id utique
naturae necessitate tanquam naturalis agens non agit;
si natura necessario egit, Patrem sibi natura gignendo
se imminuit: id quod non magis potuit Deus facere,
quam seipsum negare; non igitur nisi decreto ac libera
voluntate sua gignere potuit.[46]

'God has no need of propagation,' that is the cen-
tral thought of this paragraph of the *Of Christian
Doctrine*, and, in a very different setting, it is part
of the thought of Lactantius that God, being immortal, needs neither succession nor difference of
sex:

quid est autem a deo tam remotum quam id opus, quod
ipse ad propagandam subolem mortalibus tribuit et quod
sine substantia corporali nullum potest esse? dii ergo
si sunt inmortales et aeterni, quid opus est altero
sexu — nimirum ut generent? ipsa progenie quid opus
est, cum successione non egeant qui semper sunt futuri?
nam profecto in hominibus ceterisque animantibus di-
versitas sexus et coitio et generatio nullam habet aliam
rationem nisi ut omnia genera uiuentium, quoniam sunt
condicione mortalitatis obitura, mutua possint successione seruari, deo autem, qui est sempiternus, neque
alter sexus neque successio necessaria est. dicet aliquis
'ut habeat uel ministros uel in quos possit ipse dominari.' quid igitur sexu opus est feminino, cum deus, qui
est omnipotens ut uocatur, sine usu et opera feminae
possit filios procreare?[47]

'God has no need of succession or of the other sex; He can create alone,' is the essence of Lactantius' thought,[48] and in the fourth book he emphasizes it again, this time with reference to Christ:

qui audit dei filium dici, non debet tantum nefas mente concipere, ut existimet ex conubio ac permixtione feminae alicuius deum procreasse, quod non facit nisi animal corporale mortique subiectum.[49]

Again, Lactantius introduces the converse of the idea that God is sexless, in his argument that the heathen divinities cannot be true gods, inasmuch as sex is attributed to them. This is part of his euhemeristic argument:

. . . ex duobus sexibus alter fortior ist, alter infirmior; robustiores enim mares sunt, feminae inbecilliores. inbecillitas autem non cadit in deum, ergo nec feminae sexus. huic additur superioris argumenti extrema illa conclusio, ut dii non sint, quoniam in diis et feminae sunt.[50]

Milton's emphasis is on the fact that God needs no propagation whatever, while Lactantius, although he states that God needs no succession, lays stress on the idea that He can obtain that succession without the necessity of any female element. This difference in emphasis is partly also one in era: Lactantius, who was not born a Christian but was converted when he was well along in life,[51] was doubtless brought up on the standard pagan myths, and the idea of female deities, which he so stoutly combats, was certainly familiar to him. But, in spite of this evident difference in the turn of the thought, the responsibility for Milton's treating the idea at all seems to lie with Lactantius.

Mr. Leach, in his article, points out the likeness between the views of Lactantius, as expressed in the second book of the *Divine Institutes*, and those of Milton in the fifth book of *Paradise Lost*, as to the position of Christ in the Trinity.[52] It is with great diffidence that I approach any discussion of this subject; only a theologian, trained in the use of such terms as οὐσία, ὑπόστασις, and ὁμοούσιον, should attempt to pass judgment on a question involving anything as complicated as Arianism.

Mr. Leach says that the views of Lactantius are 'not far short of Arian,' while he calls Milton himself an Arian.[53] Why does not Lactantius fall heir to the term in its completeness? To be sure, he does not deal with the subject fully enough or with sufficient complexity for one to be able to measure his views against the eight points of Arianism drawn up by Harnack;[54] but to the lay mind Lactantius seems to fulfil the definition of

an Arian, by believing that God the Father created the Son within the limits of time, but before
the creation of the world, in which the Father used
'both His (*i. e.* the Son's) wisdom and hands.'[55]
The *Catholic Encyclopedia* thus defines the essential views of Arius:

He described the Son as a second, or inferior God,
standing midway between the First Cause and creatures;
as Himself made out of nothing, yet as making all
things else; as existing before the worlds or the ages;
and as arrayed in all divine perfections, except the one
which was their stay and foundation. God alone was
without beginning, unoriginate; the Son was originated,
and once had not existed.[56]

These views seem to tally with those of Lactantius, particularly as given in the fourth book of the
Divine Institutes. The statement in the second
book, mentioned by Mr. Leach, is very brief:

cum esset deus ad excogitandum prouidentissimus, ad
faciendum sollertissimus, antequam ordiretur hoc opus
mundi, quoniam pleni et consummati boni fons in ipso
erat, sicut est semper, ut ab eo bonum tamquam riuus
oreretur longeque proflueret, produxit similem sui spiritum, qui esset uirtutibus patris dei praeditus.[57]

The fourth book goes into more detail:

Deus igitur machinator constitutorque rerum . . .
antequam praeclarum hoc opus mundi adoriretur, sanc-

tum et incorruptibilem spiritum genuit, quem filium
nuncuparet. et quamuis alios postea innumerabiles
creauisset, quos angelos dicimus, hunc tamen solum
primogenitum diuini nominis appellatione dignatus est,
patria scilicet uirtute ac maiestate pollentem.[58]

And again, in the next chapter, Lactantius mentions the Son as having been begotten before the
world and as then helping to create it.[59] It would
seem useless to deny the Arian tendencies of Lactantius, yet the *Dictionary of Christian Biography*,
in its article on Lactantius, quotes the ecclesiastical historian, Dupin, to the effect that the Latin
Father 'seems to be of opinion that the Word was
generated in time; but it is an easy matter to
give a Catholic sense to that expression.'[60] This
appears to be something of an attempt to prove
that black is white, when one reads the words of
the Father himself, but one who is not fitted to
discuss such matters should not try to split hairs
with a theologian in attempting to prove that
Lactantius is every whit as much an Arian as
Milton himself. And that Milton was probably
such can be gathered from the article on Arianism
in the *Catholic Encyclopedia*, which singles out
Milton, along with Sir Isaac Newton, as one of the

extremely few people 'perhaps tainted' with genuine Arianism.[61]

We have heard Lactantius speak; now let us hear Milton. The passages in the fifth book of *Paradise Lost* referred to by Mr. Leach deal with the knotty theological problem of the begetting of the Son as if it were a quite simple idea, without the complexity that theologians have found, or created, in it. Both passages are in the account of primal things, as narrated to Adam by Raphael. The first is found in *Paradise Lost*, v, 577–615:

'As yet this World was not, and Chaos wild
Reigned where these heavens now roll, where Earth now
    rests
Upon her centre poised, when on a day
(For Time, though in Eternity, applied
To motion, measures all things durable
By present, past, and future), on such day
As Heaven's great year brings forth, the empyreal host
Of Angels, by imperial summons called,
Innumerable before the Almighty's throne
Forthwith from all the ends of Heaven appeared
Under their hierarchs in orders bright.
                 . . . Thus when in orbs
Of circuit inexpressible they stood,
Orb within orb, the Father Infinite,
By whom in bliss embosomed sat the Son,
Amidst, as from a flaming mount, whose top
Brightness had made invisible, thus spake: —

'"Hear, all ye Angels, Progeny of Light,
Thrones, Dominations, Princedoms, Virtues, Powers,
Hear my decree, which unrevoked shall stand!
This day have I begot whom I declare
My only Son, and on this holy hill
Him have anointed, whom ye now behold
At my right hand. Your head I him appoint,
And by myself have sworn to him shall bow
All knees in Heaven, and shall confess him Lord.
Under his great vicegerent reign abide,
United as one individual soul,
For ever happy. Him who disobeys
Me disobeys, breaks union, and, that day,
Cast out from God and blessed vision, falls
Into utter darkness, deep engulfed, his place
Ordained without redemption, without end."'

The announcement to the angels of the begetting of the Son recalls the words in Hebrews, 1, 5, 'For unto which of the angels said he at any time, Thou art my Son, this day have I begotten thee?' — a passage which is, of course, based on the similar verse in the second Psalm.[62] This conception of Milton's would be all very well, Arian though it may be, were it not for what looks like a contradiction of it, that appears a few hundred lines later, still in Raphael's narrative, in the retort of Abdiel to Satan, over the question of revolt, (*Paradise Lost*, v, 833–840):

Thyself, though great and glorious, dost thou count,
Or all angelic nature joined in one,
Equal to him, begotten Son, by whom,
As by his Word, the mighty Father made
All things, even thee, and all the Spirits of Heaven
By him created in their bright degrees,
Crowned them with glory, and to their glory named
Thrones, Dominations, Princedoms, Virtues, Powers?

If the Son was the Father's instrument in creating all things, including the angels, how could they antedate Him to the extent that His actual begetting was announced to them? Professor Masson notes this inconsistency, without, however, penetrating Milton's 'sacred reserve.' [63] Professor Saurat proposes an ingenious solution, in the application to this passage of bits of the *Book of Enoch*.[64] Unfortunately for the demonstrability of this solution, as Professor Saurat himself points out, these passages from *Enoch* were not in the fragment of Syncellus, and were therefore not available in Milton's day.[65] But, impossible as it is to say that Milton borrowed from *Enoch*, still the parallel is too close to be passed over in silence.

The teaching of *Enoch* as to the preëxistence of the Son is thus summed up by Dr. R. H. Charles: 'He (not his name) has been chosen and hidden

in God's presence from before creation and unto
eternity; the Most High has preserved him and
revealed him to the elect; his glory is for ever and
ever.' [66]   There are several significant verses:

Yea, before the sun and the signs were created,
Before the stars of the heaven were made,
His name was named before the Lord of Spirits.[67]

And for this reason hath he been chosen and hidden
    before Him,
Before the creation of the world and for evermore.[68]

Most striking of all is the verse:

For from the beginning the Son of Man was hidden,
And the Most High preserved him in the presence of
    His might,
And revealed him to the elect.[69]

If this last verse had been included by Syncellus,
we should have an explanation of the puzzle of
Milton's apparent antedating of the Son by the
angels.

As things are, however, we must look to some
other source of rabbinical lore than *Enoch*. Professor H. A. Wolfson has very kindly furnished
me with a passage bearing on this point, which
shows that the *Enoch* tradition survived, even
when the book itself was not available. The passage is from the *Pesikta Rabbati:* [70]

What is the meaning of the verse 'In thy light shall we see light' (Psalms, 36, 10)? Now, what light is it that the assembly of Israel is looking forward to? It is the light of the Messiah, for it is written, 'And God saw the light, that it was good' (Genesis, 1, 4). This teaches us that the Holy One, blessed be He, had foreseen the Messiah and his deeds before the world was created and He hid the Messiah under His throne of glory where he is to remain until his appointed time. [Said Satan to the Holy One, blessed be He, O Master of the universe, the light that is hidden under Thy throne of glory, whom is it for? God answered, For him who is destined to cause thee to turn back and retire in shame.] Said Satan, Pray, show him to me. Said God, Come and behold him. As soon as he beheld him, he trembled and fell upon his face and said, Verily this is the Messiah who is destined to cast me and all the principalities of the nations of the world into Gehenna.

Professor Wolfson goes on to say, 'The *Pesikta Rabbati* was not available in printed form before 1657. But the same passage occurs with some slight variations in a later compilation known as *Yalkut Shime'oni*, which was printed several times before the end of the sixteenth century.' This hiding of the Messiah under the throne of glory would explain how He could both exist before the angels and be unknown to them until the given occasion of the Father's announcement of Him.

One could hardly claim, without a thorough knowledge of Milton's Semitic scholarship, that he had read this given passage in the *Yalkut Shime 'oni.* A recent book, *Milton's Semitic Studies*, by Professor H. F. Fletcher,[71] does not consider this point, and there remains only the sheer guess that this rabbinical tradition had reached Milton and had led him to introduce the proclamation of the begetting of the Son comparatively late in the scheme of things. Whether Milton had happened on the passage in question in his reading, or had found the idea in some Latin compilation of Hebrew excerpts, or whether the tradition had reached him orally can be only a matter of conjecture, without definite rabbinical knowledge as a background.

But, whatever the history of Milton's version of the begetting of the Son, the consensus of opinion seems to be that he was a real Arian. However, in the Arianism of Lactantius and Milton there is a fundamental difference of approach: Lactantius was concerned with impressing an unbelieving audience with the close connection between the Father and the Son, Milton with making a distinction between them that was not generally acceptable in his time. Arianism was merely

incidental to the belief of Lactantius, but with
Milton it was a point to be proved in the face of
opposition.

In the third book of *Paradise Lost* Milton speaks
of the Son as 'of all creation first,' [72] and in *Of
Christian Doctrine* he says, 'Hoc constat . . . Filium
. . . Verbi sive Sermonis sub nomine, in principio
extitisse, rerum creatarum primum fuisse, per
quem deinde caetera omnia tam in coelo quam in
terra sunt facta.' [73] Neither Lactantius nor Milton
claims the Son to have existed from all eternity,
but from a given point of time, before the creation
of the world. In fact, Milton takes pains to emphasize this belief, that the Son has not existed from
eternity:

Nam qui ab aeterno genitus est, eum certe Pater
genuit nunquam; quod enim ab aeterno est factum, id
nunquam fiebat; quem Pater ab aeterno genuit, eum
profecto adhuc gignit; quem adhuc gignit, is nondum
est genitus, nondum ergo Filius: quae enim actio ini-
tium non habet, ea neque habet finem.[74]

Milton seems, then, to have shared the Arian
views of Lactantius as to the subordination of the
Son to the Father in the Trinity. That, however,
is no claim that, without the Latin Father, Milton

would have followed more orthodox paths of thought. In the first place, Milton was perfectly capable of arriving at this point of view by himself; in the second place, there were plenty of other sources through which Arianism could have reached him. Neither would Milton, with his fiercely independent belief in the individual's right to his own thought, have ever felt the need for the backing of an accepted Father of the Church before daring to broach such a subject. But it does seem quite possible that Lactantius, if that author were read in Milton's school days, was the first patristic writer in whom he found explicitly stated the Arian views that he must already have heard referred to, possibly fulminated against, from some pulpit or in some book or pamphlet. Arianism itself he must have heard of before he came to read Lactantius, but the *Divine Institutes* may well have been the first orderly and eloquent setting forth of that point of view to reach Milton's attention.

There is one very curious point connected with belief in the Son on which Lactantius and Milton agree, where the Latin Father may well have been Milton's direct source. Both speak of the audi-

bility of the Word of God, the Λόγος, as an actual
fact. Now Lactantius was not the originator of
this thought, but the Greek Fathers, 'the great
majority' of whom, says the *Catholic Encyclopedia*,
'understood λόγος not of the mental thought, but
of the uttered word.' [75] The references in the *Encyclopedia*, however, emphasize not so much the
audibility of the Word as its physical production.
Milton knew such Fathers as Basil, Cyprian, Eusebius, Justin Martyr, and Gregory of Nyssa, all of
whom he quotes in his *Commonplace Book*. Of
these Basil wrote a homily, entitled *Homilia in
illud, In Principio erat Verbum*, in which he makes
the statement, 'Περὶ γὰρ τοῦ Μονογενοῦς διαλεγόμενός
σοι, Λόγον εἶπεν αὐτόν.' [76] But on this same page
Basil speaks of the word as proceeding from the
mind of God, not from His mouth, as in Lactantius.[77] It is this emphasis on the actual audibility
of the Λόγος that makes Lactantius seem the probable source of this idea for Milton, rather than the
Greek Fathers.

The literalness of this point of view, which converts into the heard that which is inapprehensible
to the ear, is more closely akin to the practical
spirit of Lactantius than it is to Milton's. Lac-

tantius conceives of a God that one would respect
rather than adore. Much has been said of the
resemblance of Milton's delineation of God to a
sort of superior schoolmaster, but that is surely
not his final conception so much as it is the unfor-
tunate result of using the Deity as a character in
the epic. But Lactantius' treatment of the subject, his conception of the Creator as merely moral
and all-powerful, is as inferior to Milton's 'Om-
nipotent, Immutable, Immortal, Infinite,' [78] as
Milton's portrayal is in turn unsatisfying beside
Dante's 'L'amor che muove il Sole e l'altre stelle.'

It is in *Of Christian Doctrine* that Milton states
the literal audibility of the Λόγος as uttered by
God, making the Son on this account of a different
essence from God the Father. He is referring to
the text, 'In the beginning was the Word,' [79] and
continues:

In principio, inquit; non ab aeterno. *Sermo:* audi-
bilis ergo: at Deus, ut invisibilis est, ita et est inaudi-
bilis. Joan. v. 37. non igitur ejusdem essentiae sermo
cum Deo.[80]

Lactantius speaks at much greater length and
more explicitly:

sed tamen quoniam spiritus et sermo diuersis partibus
proferuntur, siquidem spiritus naribus, ore sermo pro-

cedit, magna inter hunc dei filium ceterosque angelos differentia est. illi enim ex deo taciti spiritus exierunt, quia non ad doctrinam dei tradendam, sed ad ministerium creabantur. ille uero cum sit et ipse spiritus, tamen cum uoce ac sono ex dei ore processit sicut uerbum, ea scilicet ratione, quia uoce eius ad populum fuerat usurus, id est quod ille magister futurus esset doctrinae dei et caelestis arcani ad homines perferendi. ipsum primo locutus est, ut per eum ad nos loqueretur et ille uocem dei ac uoluntatem nobis reuelaret. merito igitur sermo ac uerbum dei dicitur, quia deus procedentem de ore suo uocalem spiritum, quem non utero, sed mente conceperat, inexcogitabili quadam maiestatis suae uirtute ac potentia in effigiem, quae proprio sensu et sapientia uigeat, conprehendit; et alios item spiritus suos in angelos figurauit. . . . nostrae uoces licet aurae misceantur atque uanescant, tamen plerumque permanent litteris conprehensae: quanto magis dei uocem credendum est et manere in aeternum et sensu ac uirtute comitari, quam de deo patre tamquam riuus de fonte traduxerit! quodsi quis miratur ex deo deum prolatione uocis ac spiritus potuisse generari, si sacras uoces prophetarum cognouerit, desinet profecto mirari.[81]

The difference that Lactantius makes between the angels, which proceeded from God as silent spirits, and the audible Word coming forth from the mouth of God with voice and sound; the idea that Christ issued forth in voice because He in turn was to use His own voice as a teacher of heavenly knowledge; the thought of God 'produced from God by a putting forth of the voice and breath' [82] — all these conceptions must have caught Milton's eye, may even have lingered in his memory, because of their very strangeness. The Scripture, however, is all that he ever cites as authority in his definition of his own faith, and this is accordingly no place for him to mention Lactantius, even if he remembered the passage explicitly. He may, of course, have long since forgotten the exact place where he ran across this idea, which lay dormant in his memory until he needed it. But whether realized or unrealized, it is quite possible that it is Lactantius that lies behind the brief statement in *Of Christian Doctrine*, 'The Word, therefore the Word was audible.'

Milton's strictures on the amusements of the Roman people in the fourth book of *Paradise Regained* may show a reminiscence of his reading in Lactantius. The Christian Father is full of local color: he speaks of the horrors of the persecutions and tortures of the Christians as if he had been an eyewitness;[83] he draws on the institution of slavery for his comparisons of the Christian who recants under the torture to a runaway slave;[84] he mentions the practice of exposing children to death;[85] but there is nothing that speaks more eloquently of the times in which Lactantius lived than his repeated emphasis on the wickedness of gladiatorial games. He mentions them in connection with the Roman drama, and it is this combination of the gory shows of the arena with the 'effeminate' stage that Milton may have remembered in *Paradise Regained*, iv, 132–142:

> That people, victor once, now vile and base,
> Deservedly made vassal . . .
>   . . . first ambitious grown
> Of triumph, that insulting vanity;
> Then cruel, by their sports to blood inured
> Of fighting beasts, and men to beasts exposed;
> Luxurious by their wealth, and greedier still,
> And from the daily scene effeminate.

But why should the stage be called effeminate in its effects? Lactantius has an answer, in his condemnation of spectacles. First, the gladiatorial shows are objects of his censure, and he describes the wolfish ways of the crowd at a combat in the arena:

quaero nunc an possint pii et iusti homines esse qui constitutos sub ictu mortis ac misericordiam deprecantes non tantum patiuntur occidi, sed et flagitant feruntque ad mortem crudelia et inhumana suffragia nec uulneribus satiati nec cruore contenti. quin etiam percussos iacentesque repeti iubent et cadauera ictibus dissipari, ne quis illos simulata morte deludat. irascuntur etiam pugnantibus, nisi celeriter e duobus alter occisus est, et tamquam humanum sanguinem sitiant, oderunt moras. alios illis conpares dari poscunt recentiores, ut quam primum oculos suos satient. hac consuetudine inbuti humanitatem perdiderunt.[86]

'They have lost their humanity': so Lactantius sums up the watchers of these spectacles. But he has little better to say of the influence of the drama of the day, which he considers immoral, debasing, and effeminate:

in scaenis quoque nescio an sit corruptela uitiosior. nam et comicae fabulae de stupris uirginum loquuntur aut amoribus meretricum, et quo magis sunt eloquentes qui flagitia illa finxerunt, eo magis sententiarum elegantia persuadent et facilius inhaerent audientium memoriae uersus numerosi et ornati ... et incesta regum malorum et coturnata scelera demonstrant. histrionum quoque inpudicissimi motus quid aliut nisi libidines et docent et instigant? quorum eneruata corpora et in muliebrum incessum habitumque mollita inpudicas feminas inhonestis gestibus mentiuntur.[87]

This is not all that Lactantius has to say,[88] but it is enough to show his attitude and his emphasis on the enervating and effeminate influence of the plays, both comedy and tragedy. Milton shows his knowledge of this very chapter by his entry in the *Commonplace Book* on it,[89] and by his remark that, in the next chapter,[90] Lactantius would take away music also from the world. Thus we have in both Lactantius and Milton a coupling of gladiatorial combats and the drama as vicious spectacles, and an emphasis in both on the effeminacy of plays, and all this occurs in a chapter of Lactantius that Milton himself testifies to having known.

One could hardly ask for a clearer case of influence of the one on the other, were it not for the fact that Lactantius probably drew on Tertullian's *De Spectaculis* for some of his points, and that Milton likewise knew this treatise, as he shows by two entries in the *Commonplace Book*.[91] One of these precedes the entry on Lactantius just mentioned, both in position on the page and in time of entry.[92] Tertullian also treats of the two types of Roman spectacle, the combat and the play, but not in the same chapter; he, too, mentions the shamefulness of a man dressed in woman's clothes,[93] and he even uses the word *effeminati* in connection with acting.[94] Thus Tertullian, as

well as Lactantius, may have been drawn upon
by Milton. The balance between the two seems
very nearly even, except that there may be an
inclination of the scales toward Lactantius, because, instead of scattering his references to these
various influences, as does Tertullian, he sums
them all up in one striking chapter, thus unifying
his effect on the mind of a reader.

A point, according to Mr. Leach, on which Milton may have borrowed actual information from
Lactantius is in the mention of Hermes Trismegistus in *Il Penseroso*, 88.[95] Mr. Leach might also
have brought up the mention of the same myste-
rious personage, or rather, galaxy of personages, in
the *De Idea Platonica quemadmodum Aristoteles
Intellexit*, 32–34:

> Non ille trino gloriosus nomine
> Ter magnus Hermes (ut si arcani sciens)
> Talem reliquit Isidis cultoribus.

This use of Hermes Trismegistus in an academic
exercise at Cambridge places the knowledge of his
name earlier than the more familiar reference in
Il Penseroso. Professor Fletcher assumes that it
was at Cambridge and by way of some Semitic
authority that Milton became familiar with this

Hermes.[96] But, since no evidence is adduced to prove that the knowledge of Trismegistus was gained at Cambridge and through Hebrew, there is in this argument nothing to interfere with the contention of Mr. Leach, that this knowledge was derived from Lactantius and probably at St. Paul's.

No reader of Lactantius can fail to be struck with the use he makes of the supposed philosopher, priest, and king, a man raised to a god, called Thoth by the Egyptians and identified with Hermes by the Greeks.[97] The *Divine Institutes*, in particular, are full of references to this Hermes, references which, together with quotations from the various Sibyls, are used by the author as prophecies of Christ and testimonies to the truth of Christianity from authorities that his pagan audience would accept. Samuel Brandt, in his edition of Lactantius, lists over thirty quotations from Hermes Trismegistus, cited by name, which were drawn from the *Poimandres*, the *Asclepius*, and from various fragments.[98]

To Lactantius, as to the rest of antiquity, 'thrice-great Hermes' was a real person, who was deified by the Egyptians because of his benefits to men,[99]

and whose works could supply a Father of the
Church with most convenient prophecies.   It
would have been a shock and a painful surprise to
Lactantius to be informed by the latest editor of
the *Hermetica* that 'Hermes Trismegistus' was
merely a blanket name assumed by a variety of
neo-Platonic writers between A.D. 200 and 300, or
thereabout.[100] Mr. Walter Scott would have an interesting tale to tell Lucius Caelius Firmianus Lactantius, of little groups of 'seekers after God,' scattered through Egypt, and consisting of a teacher
and his disciples, whose talks, real or imaginary,
we still have recorded to-day in the *Hermetica*.[101]
The teachers, in most cases, assumed in their
writings the name of Hermes Trismegistus, while
their pupils were Tat, Asclepius, or Ammon.   The
Hellenistic veneration for authority and tradition
led to the assumption of this name: the master of
their master, Plato, was Pythagoras, and it was
believed that both Plato and Pythagoras had
studied in Egypt, in the schools of the priests, who
had in turn derived their wisdom from the ancient
books ascribed to the authorship of the god Thoth
or Hermes.   The motive for borrowing the name
of Hermes Trismegistus from antiquity, says Mr.

Scott, 'must have been similar to that which made a Jew write a *Book of Daniel*, or a *Book of Enoch*, instead of a book of his own.' [102] And again, 'A piece of writing to which little attention might be paid if it only bore the name of some obscure Ammonius, would carry more weight if it professed to reveal the secret teaching of Hermes Trismegistus.' [103] Lactantius, then, did not know the true inwardness of the writings he was continually quoting, but that lack of knowledge does not detract from, but rather adds to the interest aroused in the reader to know more of this unfamiliar authority.

Milton could not have escaped this same interest, as he read the *Divine Institutes*, and Mr. Leach asks, 'whether it was not from Lactantius that Milton first heard of the "thrice great Hermes."' [104] It appears that this is not an easily answered question, when one stops to consider that even the poem on the Platonic Idea tells us no more of the extent of Milton's information on Hermes Trismegistus than that he was an Egyptian sage. And also, there are many other sources from which Milton might have derived this very slender knowledge.

In the first place, Hermes Trismegistus is mentioned by other Fathers of the Church than Lactantius. Tertullian calls him 'Mercurius ille Trismegistus magister omnium Physicorum,'[105] Clement of Alexandria gives an account of his works,[106] and Augustine, in the *City of God*, devotes three chapters to Hermes' opinions on daemons.[107]   And Milton himself testifies to his knowledge of two of these works by quoting them in the *Commonplace Book*.[108]   Cicero also identifies him, in his discussion of the five Mercuries, although without using the characteristic epithet, 'Trismegistus.'[109]   Milton's edition of Justin Martyr included Hermes, according to Professor Hanford,[110] and this volume would, of course, be a sure source for gaining knowledge of the work of Trismegistus. Whether Justin or Lactantius would be read first is part of the more general question, whether or not Dean Colet's list of Christian authors was read at St. Paul's. On the score of general probability, it seems likely that Lactantius would come first in Milton's reading, but there is no denying the other possibility of Justin's priority.

Professor Thorndike shows Hermes Trismegistus to have been one of the great names for

mediaeval scientists and pseudo-scientists to con-
jure with, whether to invoke his authority in as-
tronomy, magic, or alchemy, or merely to name
him as a source of wisdom in general. Thus Professor Thorndike explains the connection of Trismegistus with magic:

Assuming as these writings (*i.e.* all 'oracular and
mystic compositions') do to disclose the secrets of ancient priesthoods and to publish what should not be
revealed to the vulgar crowd, they may be confidently
expected to embody a great deal of superstition and
magic along with the expositions of mystic theolo-
gies.' [111]

Professor Thorndike devotes a whole chapter to
'Hermetic Books in the Middle Ages,' [112] which
shows how widespread the great name of Hermes
Trismegistus was in mediaeval times. Is not the
seventeenth century too near the interest in as-
trology and alchemy for this name to be lost to
general scholarly knowledge? Sir Francis Bacon
cites 'the ancient Hermes' as if his name would be
quite familiar to his readers. [113] Purchas also, in the
Pilgrimage, gives a long description of Trismegistus
and his works, [114] referring to the passages in both
Lactantius and Augustine.

With the 'writings of Trismegistus' so well known from the Middle Ages, it seems hardly safe to claim that Milton's initial knowledge of Hermes came from Lactantius, even if he read the Church Father as early as at St. Paul's. The name of Trismegistus may still have been in the air, although his value as an authority must have declined since mediaeval times. But however the mere name may have reached Milton, it does seem possible that it was in Lactantius or in the 1636 edition of Justin Martyr that for the first time he ran across actual excerpts from the Hermetic writings, thus increasing his knowledge of and interest in Trismegistus, so that it was more than a bare name he referred to in connecting Hermes Trismegistus and Plato in *Il Penseroso*.

There are instances of resemblance between the two authors that cannot be considered as conclusive, because of the inevitability of the thought or the likelihood of other sources. For example, Milton says of Socrates, in *Paradise Regained*, iii, 97, 'For truth's sake suffering death unjust,' while Lactantius, in an attack on the indifference of Cicero toward establishing a true religion, addresses him in these words: 'sed nimirum Socratis

carcerem times ideoque patrocinium ueritatis sus-
cipere non audes.' [115] There is nothing strange or
startling in connecting the idea of Socrates with
the advocacy of truth, and Lactantius and Milton
and a hundred others might have made their respective statements without a glance into the
works of their predecessors. Yet, on the other hand,
there is no reason why Lactantius' remark may
not have made its impression on Milton's mind
and have reappeared in this verse. With no de-
cisive evidence to settle the point, it must remain
debatable.

Another moot point is that of the sheer stupidity
of those who forsake the worship of God to serve
idols. Again there is nothing new in this thought;
the vanity of idolatry as a theme throughout the
Old Testament is too familiar to need citation.
But it is interesting to see how closely parallel are
the words of Milton and the Church Father. In
Paradise Lost, xii, 115–120, we read:

> . . . Oh, that men
> (Canst thou believe?) should be so stupid grown,
> While yet the Patriarch lived who scaped the Flood,
> As to forsake the living God, and fall
> To worship their own work in wood and stone
> For gods!

Here is the corresponding passage in Lactantius:

equidem sicut oportet de summa rerum saepenumero
cogitans admirari soleo, maiestatem dei singularis quae
continet regitque omnia in tantam uenisse obliuionem,
ut quae sola debeat coli, sola potissimum neclegatur,
homines autem ipsos ad tantam caecitatem esse deduc-
tos, ut uero ac uiuo deo mortuos praeferant, terrenos
autem sepultosque in terra ei qui fundator ipsius terrae
fuit.[116]

It is true that both poet and Latin Father are
discussing not merely idolatry but the apostasy of
those who have known the true God: 'as to forsake
the living God,' says Milton, while with Lactantius it is 'ut uero ac uiuo deo mortuos praeferant.'
The shadow of the Bible falls across both passages,
and particularly across the words, 'the living God,'
so that one can say no more than that it is perfectly possible that the passage from Lactantius
arose in Milton's mind, along with the Bible, when
he wrote his words.

There is a single passage in Milton's Latin
poems that may have drawn its material from
Lactantius, if the *De Ave Phoenice* can be assumed
to be the work of the Latin Father, whether written in his Christian or pre-Christian days.[117] There
is no necessity for entering here into the com-

plexities of the controversy whether this Latin
poem should or should not be attributed to Lactantius, since the sixteenth- and seventeenth-
century editions of the Father's works, up to the
time of Milton's death, included the poem without
questioning its genuineness.[118] The first seventeenth-century edition in the Harvard College
Library that does not include *The Phoenix* is the
Oxford edition of 1684, published after Milton's
death.

Milton has three passages concerning the legend
of the Phoenix,[119] but the only one that shows the
possible influence of Lactantius is that from the
Epitaphium Damonis, 185–189, in the description
of the cups presented to Milton by the admiring
Manso:

> In medio Rubri Maris unda, et odoriferum ver,
> Littora longa Arabum, et sudantes balsama sylvae;
> Has inter Phoenix, divina avis, unica terris,
> Caeruleùm fulgens diversicoloribus alis,
> Auroram vitreis surgentem respicit undis.

There are two passages from Lactantius which
bear on this one of Milton's. The first is from the
De Ave Phoenice, 31–42:

> Hoc nemus, hos lucos auis incolit unica Phoenix,
>   Unica, sed uiuit morte refecta sua.

Paret et obsequitur Phoebo memoranda satelles:
  Hoc natura parens munus habere dedit.
Lutea cum primum surgens Aurora rubescit,
  Cum primum rosea sidera luce fugat,
Ter quater illa pias inmergit corpus in undas,
  Ter quater e uiuo gurgite libat aquam.
Tollitur ac summo considit in arboris altae
  Vertice, quae totum despicit una nemus,
Et conuersa nouos Phoebi nascentis ad ortus
  Expectat radios et iubar exoriens.

There are two details in the pair of descriptions
which tally exactly, the use of the word *unica*,
which Lactantius even repeats, and the bird's
waiting for the dawn. The second bit from *The
Phoenix* paints the creature with a bewildering
array of colors, so that it far outshines the peacock
and the pheasant, to which it is compared:

Principio color est, quali est sub sidere Cancri
  Mitia quod corium punica grana tegit,
Qualis inest foliis quae fert agreste papauer,
  Cum pandit uestes Flora rubente solo.
Hoc humeri pectusque decens uelamine fulget,
  Hoc caput, hoc ceruix summaque terga nitent.
Caudaque porrigitur fuluo distincta metallo,
  In cuius maculis purpura mixta rubet.
Alarum pennas insignit desuper iris,
  Pingere ceu nubem desuper acta solet.
Albicat insignis mixto uiridante zmaragdo
  Et puro cornu gemmea cuspis hiat.

Ingentes oculi, credas geminos hyacinthos,
    Quorum de medio lucida flamma micat.
Aptata est rutilo capiti radiata corona
    Phoebei referens uerticis alta decus.
Crura tegunt squamae fuluo distincta metallo,
    Ast ungues roseo tinguit honore color.
Effigies inter pauonis mixta figuram
    Cernitur et pictam Phasidis inter auem.[120]

The general effect of this kaleidoscopically brilliant assortment of colors may be what Milton
had in mind in speaking of the 'diversicoloribus
alis,' or he might be following Lactantius even
more closely, remembering the iridescence of the
wings themselves in the Latin.[121]

But this cannot at once be declared a clear case
of reminiscence, without considering other Latin
sources of information about the phoenix. There
is Lactantius' own source, Ovid, fragments of
whose work are scattered through the fourth-
century poem. Brandt has listed these uses of Ovid
by Lactantius,[122] but, curiously enough, only one
of the Ovidian details which Lactantius reproduces
has any possible connection with Milton. That is
the use of *unica* in *Amores*, ii, 6, 54:

Illic innocui late pascuntur olores
    Et vivax phoenix, unica semper avis.

Since this is merely an isolated mention, rather than an extended account of the phoenix, and nothing else is added by way of description, it seems probable that Milton took this actually Ovidian word along with the other bits of Lactantius' version, instead of going back to the Father's source. The word *unica* is in a way inevitable for the phoenix, and its use alone would be insufficient evidence of Milton's remembrance of either Lactantius or Ovid, but the apparent survival of other particulars from the Latin Father, and his emphasis on *unica* by his repetition of it corroborates the case for him rather than for Ovid.

But there is still another poet who uses the word *unicus*, and that is Claudian. In the second panegyric on Stilicho, he compares the gathering of the military chiefs to behold the glory of the consul to the flocking of the birds to look upon the phoenix, and he says:

> sic ubi fecunda reparavit morte inventam
> et patrios idem cineres collectaque portat
> unguibus ossa piis Nilique ad litora tendens
> unicus extremo Phoenix procedit ab Euro.[123]

But in this passage in Claudian, as in Ovid, there are none of the supporting details that are found in Lactantius, and the case for the influence of the *De Consulatu Stilichonis* is on exactly the same level of probability as that for the *Amores*. Even if Milton took the word *unicus* from Claudian, he was drawing indirectly on Lactantius, since Claudian is considered to be imitating the Latin Father in this poem.[124]

There is a whole poem by Claudian on the phoenix, however, which must be examined for Miltonic suggestions. In the twenty-first line we read,

> antevolant Zephyros pinnae, quas caerulus ambit
> flore color sparsoque super ditescit in auro.[125]

The word *caeruleum* may have been recalled by Milton from this *caerulus*, or he may have taken it from Pliny, who gives, in the *Natural History*, as brilliantly colored a description of the bird as the one in Lactantius:

> Aquilae narratur magnitudine, auri fulgore circa colla, cetero purpureus, caeruleam roseis caudam pennis distinguentibus, cristis fauces, caputque plumeo apice honestante.[126]

Or again, the memories of the two passages probably coalesced in Milton's mind without the conscious effort of recollection, leaving him merely with the unanalyzed realization that *caeruleum* was the inevitable word for his purpose. Professor Osgood, in his study, *The Classical Mythology of Milton's English Poems*,[127] mentions also the account of the brilliant plumage by Herodotus,[128] but the colors there are gold and ruby, and there is nothing of the sky-blue that is found in Milton, Claudian, and Pliny.

There is one particular in which Milton and Lactantius agree which does not occur in Claudian, in Pliny, or in Herodotus, and that is the fact that the phoenix is sitting on its tree in the paradisal grove, awaiting the dawn. Milton says, 'Auroram vitreis surgentem respicit undis,' while Lactantius is still more explicit about the time:

> Lutea cum primum surgens Aurora rubescit,
>   Cum primum rosea sidera luce fugat.

The bird, be it noticed, is still apparently in the prime of its strength and beauty in both poems; it has not yet reached the end of one of its cycle of lives, when it is to re-create itself, as is the case in Claudian, where occurs the closest parallel to the waiting for the dawn. There the dying phoenix is represented as greeting the sun just before the kindling of the renewing fires, and the setting is changed:

> Hic sedet et blando Solem clangore salutat
> debilior miscetque preces ac supplice cantu
> praestatura novas vires incendia poscit.[129]

The greeting to the risen Sun-god is not the same thing as the waiting for his rising; accordingly, there is no clash between Claudian and Lactantius in this matter.

It is not a simple decision to determine from which of these numerous sources Milton drew his earliest picture of the phoenix. Probably this is a tissue of recollections of more than one author, but the pattern imposed on the whole seems to be that of Lactantius. There are four significant particulars in Milton to be considered: the use of the words *unica* and *caeruleum;* the mingling of various colors in the bird's tropically brilliant plumage; and the phoenix's waiting for the dawn. Ovid, it appears at once, is the least important possibility as a source, since he could have contributed only the word *unica.* Pliny comes next, offering both a description of the bright plumage and the possible recollection of the word *caeruleum.* Claudian and Lactantius, the final claimants, are almost evenly matched, since each of them presents a different three of the four details, but Lactantius seems the more probable source, since all his bits of information occur in the same poem, within a hundred lines of each other, while Claudian's important details are divided between two poems. Again, the word *caerulus* in Claudian is less significant than the bird's expectation of the dawn, which occurs in Lactantius, since sky-blue is one of the stock poetical colors, and would almost inevitably be brought into a Latin poem, if one were decking out the phoenix in rainbow array. And since Claudian was drawing on Lactantius, there is every reason why there should be a correspondence between them as to details. These, then, are the reasons for considering Lactantius mainly responsible for the plan of Milton's drawing of the phoenix in the *Epitaphium Damonis:* Lactantius' double emphasis on the word *unica*, which would give Milton a twofold chance of remembering it; the description of the exotically bright plumage; the bird's awaiting the dawn; and the important factor, that all these items of description occur within the same poem, thus unifying the impression on the reader. There is no reason why frag-

mentary bits of Ovid, of Pliny, or of Claudian
may not have drifted into Milton's consciousness
and have left their mark on the poem, but there
seems to be every reason to believe that the pattern of the whole passage is Lactantian.

Where, then, has this study of the relations between Lactantius and Milton brought us? Where
but to a cumulative impression of a very real
connection between the two writers? All this evidence must be taken as a whole, as well as considered in its individual parts, for there is no single
bit, not even the passages connected with the
Areopagitica or the *Epitaphium Damonis*, on which
one can put one's finger and say, 'Here and nowhere else did Milton certainly get this information, or this idea.' But there are too many instances of highly probable influence for one to be
able to disregard Lactantius as one of Milton's
minor sources. This influence is slight and subtle,
rather than obvious; it affects minute points, for
the most part, a line here and a turn of thought
there. It is not, in short, one that he who runs
may read. But there seems to be no room for
doubt that Milton knew Lactantius thoroughly,
that he stopped to weigh the Latin Father's words,

and that the results of these ponderings affected the conceptions and the expression of passages in Milton's poetry and prose, Latin as well as English, both early and late in his career.

Lactantius, with his zeal for purity and discipline, had much in common with Milton's own genuine Puritanism. Much in the Lactantian philosophy must have been congenial from the start, while the most polished prose of the fourth century would of itself recommend its writer to Milton, the greatest Latin stylist of his own day. When one considers that Milton may have known Lactantius from his very school days, there is nothing surprising in finding that the seventeenth-century poet admired and respected the fourth-century Father, to the extent of drawing on him for entries in the *Commonplace Book* and for citations in the prose. As for the influence on Milton's poetry, it is theological conceptions and mythological information that he draws from Lactantius, and who shall say whether he borrowed consciously, or whether the *Divine Institutes* and *The Phoenix* had not become part of the very texture of Milton's memory?

APPENDICES

APPENDICES

A*

PASSAGES FROM LACTANTIUS SUMMARIZED IN MILTON'S *COMMONPLACE BOOK*

1. *A Commonplace Book of John Milton* (ed. A. J. Horwood), p. 1 (p. 4 of Milton's paging).

   Div. Insts., *CSEL*, vol. 19, Bk. V, chap. 7, §§ 3–6, 8–10, pp. 419–421.

   . . . magnae hoc disputationis est, cur a deo, cum iustitiam terrae daret, sit retenta diuersitas: quod et alio loco declaraui et ubicumque opportune inciderit explicabitur. nunc designare id breuissime satis est, uirtutem aut cerni non posse, nisi habeat uitia contraria, aut non esse perfectam, nisi *exerceatur* aduersis. hanc enim deus bonorum ac malorum uoluit esse distantiam, ut qualitatem boni ex malo sciamus, item mali ex bono: nec alterius ratio intellegi sublato altero potest. deus ergo non exclusit malum, *ut ratio uirtutis constare posset.* quomodo enim patientia uim suam nomenque retineret, si nihil esset quod pati cogeremur?

---

* The italics used throughout this Appendix are mine, and indicate a correspondence in wording between Lactantius and the *Commonplace Book*.

quomodo laudem mereretur deuota deo suo fides,
nisi esset aliquis qui a deo uellet auertere? . . . si
enim uirtus est malis ac uitiis fortiter repugnare,
apparet sine malo ac uitio nullam esse uirtutem.
quam deus ut absolutam perfectamque redderet,
retinuit id quod erat ei contrarium, cum quo de-
pugnare posset: agitata enim malis quatientibus
stabilitatem capit et quanto frequenter inpellitur,
tanto firmiter roboratur. haec nimirum causa effi-
cit ut quamuis sit hominibus missa iustitia, tamen
aureum saeculum non esse dicatur, quia malum
non sustulit, ut retineret diuersitatem, quae sacra-
mentum diuinae religionis continet sola.

2. *Commonplace Book*, p. 1 (p. 4 of Milton's
    paging).
    De Ira Dei, CSEL, vol. 27. ii. 1, chap. 13, §§ 13–
    25, pp. 102–104.

. . . deus cum formaret hominem ueluti simula-
crum suum, quod erat diuini opificii summum, in-
spirauit ei sapientiam soli, ut omnia imperio ac
dicioni suae subiugaret omnibusque mundi com-
modis uteretur. proposuit tamen ei et bona et
mala, quia sapientiam dedit, cuius omnis ratio in
discernendis bonis ac malis sita est. non potest

enim quisquam eligere meliora et scire quod bonum
sit, nisi sciat simul reicere ac uitare quae mala sunt.
inuicem sibi alterutra conexa sunt, ut sublato
alterutro utrumque sit tolli necesse. propositis
igitur bonis malisque tum demum opus suum
peragit sapientia et quidem bonum adpetit ad
utilitatem, malum reicit ad salutem. ergo sicut
bona innumerabilia data sunt quibus frui posset,
sic etiam mala quae caueret. nam si malum nullum
sit, nullum periculum, nihil denique quod laedere
hominem possit, tolletur omnis materia sapientiae
nec erit homini necessaria. positis enim tantummodo in conspectu bonis quid opus est cogitatione
intellectu scientia ratione, cum quocumque por-
rexerit manum, id naturae aptum et adcommoda-
tum sit? ut si quis uelit apparatissimam cenam
infantibus qui nondum sapiant adponere, utique id
adpetent singuli quo unum quemque aut impetus
aut fames aut etiam casus attraxerit, et quidquid
sumpserint, id illis erit uitale ac salubre. quid
igitur nocebit eos sicuti sunt permanere et semper
infantes ac nescios esse rerum? si autem admis-
ceas uel amara uel inutilia uel etiam uenenata, deci-
pientur utique per ignorantiam boni ac mali, nisi
accedat his sapientia per quam habeant malorum

reiectionem bonorumque dilectum. uides ergo magis propter mala opus nobis esse sapientia: quae
nisi fuissent proposita, rationale animal non esse-
mus. quod si haec ratio uera est, quam Stoici nullo
modo uidere potuerunt, dissoluitur etiam illud argumentum Epicuri. 'deus' inquit 'aut uult tollere
mala et non potest, aut potest et non uult, aut
neque uult neque potest, aut et uult et potest. si
uult et non potest, inbecillus est, quod in deum
non cadit; si potest et non uult, inuidus, quod
aeque alienum est a deo; si neque uult neque
potest, et inuidus et inbecillus est ideoque nec
deus; si et uult et potest, quod solum deo conuenit,
unde ergo sunt mala aut cur illa non tollit?' scio
plerosque philosophorum qui prouidentiam defen-
dunt, hoc argumento perturbari solere et inuitos
paene adigi ut deum nihil curare fateantur, quod
maxime quaerit Epicurus, sed nos ratione per-
specta formidolosum hoc argumentum facile dis-
soluimus. deus enim potest quidquid uelit et inbecillitas uel inuidia in eo nulla est, potest igitur
mala tollere, sed non uult; nec ideo tamen inuidus
est. idcirco enim non tollit, quia sapientiam, sicut
edocui, simul tribuit et plus est boni ac iucundita-
tis in sapientia quam in malis molestiae. sapientia

enim facit ut etiam deum cognoscamus et per eam
cognitionem inmortalitem adsequamur, quod est
summum bonum. itaque nisi prius malum agnoue-
rimus, nec bonum poterimus agnoscere. sed hoc
non uidit Epicurus nec alius quisquam, si tollantur
mala, tolli pariter sapientiam nec ulla in homine
uirtutis remanere uestigia: cuis ratio in sustinenda
et superanda malorum acerbitate consistit. ita
propter exiguum conpendium sublatorum malorum et uero et proprio nobis bono careremus.
constat igitur omnia propter hominem proposita
tam mala quam etiam bona.

3. *Commonplace Book*, p. 1 (p. 5 of Milton's
    paging).
    Div. Insts., Bk. VI, chap. 18, §§ 11–13, 17–19,
    pp. 548–550.

quin etiam caueat diligenter ne quando inimi-
cum sua culpa faciat, et si quis extiterit tam pro-
teruus, qui bono et iusto faciat iniuriam, clementer
ac moderate ferat et ultionem suam non sibi ad-
sumat, sed iudicio dei reseruet. innocentiam semper et ubique custodiat. quod praeceptum non ad
hoc tantum ualet, ut ipse iniuriam non inferat, sed
ut inlatam sibi non uindicet. sedet enim maximus

et aequissimus iudex, speculator ac testis omnium.
hunc homini praeferat, hunc malit de causa sua
pronuntiare, cuius sententiam nemo effugere potest
nec defensione cuiusquam nec gratia. ita fit ut
homo iustus contemptui sit omnibus, et quia puta-
bitur se ipsum non posse defendere, habebitur pro
segni et *inerte*. . . . non minus enim mali est referre
iniuriam quam inferre. nam unde certamina inter
homines, unde pugnae contentionesque nascuntur,
nisi quod inprobitati opposita inpatientia magnas
saepe concitat tempestates? quodsi *patientiam*, qua
uirtute nihil uerius, nihil homine dignius inueniri
potest, inprobitati opposueris, extinguetur proti-
nus, tamquam igni aquam superfuderis.

4. *Commonplace Book*, p. 4 (p. 18 of Milton's
   paging).
   De Opificio Dei, CSEL, vol. 27. ii. 1, chap. 3,
   §§ 11–18, pp. 12–13.

quaero igitur ab iis qui condicionem pecudum
suae praeferunt, quid eligant, si deus iis deferat
optionem, utrum malint, humanamne sapientiam
cum inbecillitate an pecudum firmitatem cum illa-
rum natura. scilicet non tam pecudes sunt, ut
non malint uel fragiliorem multo quam nunc est

dummodo humanam quam illam inrationabilem
firmitatem. sed uidelicet prudentes uiri neque
hominis rationem uolunt cum fragilitate neque
mutorum firmitatem sine ratione. < quid > quod
nihil est tam repugnans tamque contrarium, quod
unum quodque animal aut ratio instruat necesse
est aut condicio naturae? si naturalibus *muni-*
mentis instruatur, superuacua ratio est. quid enim
excogitabit? quid faciet? quid molietur? aut in
quo lumen illud ingenii ostendet, cum ea quae
possint esse rationis, ultro natura concedat? si
autem ratione sit praeditum, quid opus erit saepi-
mentis corporis, cum semel concessa ratio naturae
munus possit inplere? quae quidem tantum ualet
ad ornandum tuendumque hominem, ut nihil po-
tuerit maius ac melius a deo dari. denique cum et
corporis non magni homo et exiguarum uirium et
ualitudinis sit infirmae, tamen quoniam id quod
est maius accepit, et instructior est ceteris animali-
bus et ornatior. nam cum fragilis inbecillusque
nascatur, tamen et a mutis omnibus tutus est et
ea omnia quae firmiora nascuntur, etiamsi uim
caeli fortiter patiuntur, ab homine tamen tuta
esse non possunt. ita fit ut plus homini conferat
ratio quam natura mutis, quoniam in illis neque

magnitudo uirium neque firmitas corporis efficere potest quominus aut opprimantur a nobis aut nostrae subiecta sint potestati. potestne igitur aliquis cum uideat etiam boues lucas cum inmanissimis corporibus ac uiribus seruire homini, queri de opifice rerum deo, quod modicas uires, quod paruum corpus acceperit, nec beneficia in se diuina pro merito aestimat? quod est ingrati aut ut uerius loquamur, insani.

5. *Commonplace Book*, p. 21 (p. 178 of Milton's paging).

    Div. Insts., Bk. VI, chap. 6, §§ 19–20, 23, pp. 502–504.

quae sunt enim 'patriae commoda' nisi alterius ciuitatis aut gentis incommoda, id est fines propagare aliis uiolenter ereptos, *augere imperium*, vectigalia facere maiora? quae omnia non utique uirtutes, sed uirtutum sunt euersiones. in primis enim tollitur humanae societatis coniunctio, tollitur innocentia, tollitur alieni abstinentia, tollitur denique ipsa iustitia: quae discidium generis humani ferre non potest et ubicumque arma fulserint, hinc eam fugari et exterminari necesse est. . . . haec itaque ut ipsi appellant bona quisquis patriae ad-

quisiuerit, hoc est qui euersis ciuitatibus gentibus-
que deletis aerarium pecunia referserit, agros ce-
perit, ciues suos locupletiores fecerit, hic laudibus
fertur in caelum, in hoc putatur summa et perfecta
esse uirtus. qui error non modo populi et imperi-
torum, sed etiam philosophorum est, qui praecepta
quoque dant ad iniustitiam, ne stultitiae ac malitiae disciplina et auctoritas desit.

6. *Commonplace Book*, pp. 50–51 (p. 241 of Milton's paging).
   Div. Insts., Bk. VI, chap. 20, §§ 27–31, pp.
   560–561.

in scaenis quoque nescio an sit corruptela uitiosior. nam et comicae fabulae de stupris uirginum
loquuntur aut amoribus meretricum, et quo magis
sunt eloquentes qui flagitia illa finxerunt, eo magis
sententiarum elegentia persuadent et facilius inhaerent audientium memoriae uersus numerosi et
ornati. item tragicae historiae subiciunt oculis
parricidia et incesta regum malorum et coturnata
scelera demonstrant. histrionum quoque inpudicissimi motus quid aliut nisi libidines et docent
et instigant? quorum eneruata corpora et in mulie-
brem incessum habitumque mollita inpudicas femi-

nas inhonestis gestibus mentiuntur. quid de mimis
loquar corruptelarum praeferentibus disciplinam,
qui docent adulteria, dum fingunt, et simulacris
erudiunt ad uera? quid iuuenes aut uirgines faci-
ant, cum haec et fieri sine pudore et spectari liben-
ter ab omnibus cernunt? admonentur utique quid
facere possint et inflammantur libidine, quae aspectu maxime concitatur, ac se quisque pro sexu
in illis imaginibus praefigurat probantque illa, dum
rident, et adhaerentibus uitiis corruptiores ad cu-
bicula reuertuntur, nec pueri modo, quos praema-
turis uitiis imbui non oportet, sed etiam senes,
quos peccare iam non decet.

7. *Commonplace Book*, p. 51 (p. 241 of Milton's
     paging).
   Div. Insts., Bk. VI, chap. 21, §§ 1, 8, pp. 562,
     563.

Aurium uoluptas ex uocum et cantuum suaui-
tate percipitur, quae scilicet tam uitiosa est quam
oblectatio illa de qua diximus oculorum. . . . nihil
aspectu gratum sit nisi quod iuste, quod pie fieri
uideas, nihil auditu suaue nisi quod alit animam
melioremque te reddit, maximeque hic sensus non
est ad uitium detorquendus, qui nobis ideo datus
est, ut doctrinam dei percipere possemus.

B

Div. Insts., Bk. I, chap. 14, §§ 2–7, p. 53.

haec Ennii uerba sunt: 'exim Saturnus uxorem
duxit Opem. Titan, qui maior natu erat, postulat
ut ipse regnaret. ibi Vesta mater eorum et sorores
Ceres atque Ops suadent Saturno, uti de regno ne
concedat fratri. ibi Titan, qui facie deterior esset
quam Saturnus, idcirco et quod uidebat matrem
atque sorores suas operam dare uti Saturnus regnaret, concessit ei ut is regnaret. itaque pactus est
cum Saturno, uti si quid liberum uirile secus ei
natum esset, ne quid educaret. id eius rei causa
fecit, uti ad suos gnatos regnum rediret. tum
Saturno filius qui primus natus est, eum necaue-
runt. deinde posterius nati sunt gemini, Iuppiter
atque Iuno. tum Iunonem Saturno in conspectum
dedere atque Iouem clam abscondunt dantque
eum Vestae educandum celantes Saturnum. item
Neptunum clam Saturno Ops parit eumque clan-
culum abscondit. ad eundem modum tertio partu
Ops parit geminos Plutonem et Glaucam. Pluto
Latine est Dis pater, alii Orcum uocant. ibi filiam

Glaucam Saturno ostendunt, at filium Plutonem celant atque abscondunt. deinde Glauca parua emoritur. haec, ut scripta sunt, Iouis fratrumque eius stirps atque cognatio: in hunc modum nobis ex sacra scriptione traditum est.' item paulo post haec infert: 'deinde Titan postquam resciuit Saturno filios procreatos atque educatos esse clam se, seducit secum filios suos qui Titani uocantur, fratremque suum Saturnum atque Opem conprehendit eosque muro circumegit et custodiam iis apponit.' . . . reliqua historia sic contexitur: 'Iouem adultum, cum audisset patrem atque matrem custodiis circumsaeptos atque in uincula coniectos, uenisse cum magna Cretensium multitudine Titanumque ac filios eius pugna uicisse, parentes uinculis exemisse, patri regnum reddidisse atque ita in Cretam remeasse. post haec deinde Saturno sortem datam, ut caueret ne filius eum regno expelleret; illum eleuandae sortis atque effugiendi periculi gratia insidiatum Ioui, ut eum necaret; Iouem cognitis insidiis regnum sibi denuo uindicasse ac fugasse Saturnum. qui cum iactatus esset per omnes terras persequentibus armatis, quos ad eum conprehendendum uel necandum Iuppiter miserat, uix in Italia locum in quo lateret inuenit.'

C

PURCHAS AND MILTON

There are several striking resemblances between Milton and Purchas, to which Professor Lowes called my attention. These similarities open another question of influences. Did Milton get some of his information on the heathen gods, which he displayed so lavishly in the *Nativity Ode* and in the opening of *Paradise Lost*, from a contemporary travel book?

We have evidence that he not only read Purchas, but even made note of points that interested him, in two entries in the *Commonplace Book*. The first, under the heading '*Gula*,' is the third entry on page 13:[1] 'The Indians in Summatra, great gluttons, renew thire stomack by chewing an hearb call'd Arecca betula. *Parchas* (sic), tom. 1, 132.' A search for this information upon the page given by Milton will fail to disclose his citation. But the fault is not Milton's, for he simply copied the page number given in his edition of *Purchas his Pilgrimes*, which is that of 1625. The pagination of the book itself is wrong, because there are two

pages marked 132, whereas the first should be 122.
A professional faultfinder would have a hard time
hunting for mistakes in Milton, but this instance,
that looks so like an undeniable error, would be
the biggest disappointment of all.

The passage in Purchas to which Milton refers
is drawn from *A briefe Relation of Master Iohn
Davis, chiefe Pilot to the Zelanders in their East-
India Voyage, departing from Middleborough the
fifteenth of March, Anno 1598.*[2] The account, dealing with the life at the court of 'Sultan Aladin' of
Achen, is an unlovely one:

> The King . . . doth nothing all the day but eate and
> drinke, from morning to night there is no end of ban-
> quetting: and when his belly is readie to breake, then
> hee eateth *Arecca Betula*, which is a fruit like a Nutmeg,
> wrapped in a kind of leafe like *Tabacco*, with sharpe
> chalke made of Pearle Oyster-shels: chawing this it
> maketh the spittle very red . . . and procureth a mightie
> stomacke: this maketh the teeth very blacke, and they
> be the brauest that haue the blackest teeth. By this
> meanes getting againe his stomacke, he goeth with a
> fresh courage to eating. . . . Hee, his great men and
> women doe nothing but eate, drinke, and talke of Ve-
> nerie. If the Poets Fables have any shew of truth, then
> undoubtedly this King is the great *Bacchus*. For he
> holdeth all the Ceremonies of Gluttonie.

The other appearance of Purchas is in the last entry under the heading '*De Poetica*,' on page 57 of Milton's paging: 'Numidian poets, Leo Afer in *Purchas*, tom 2. 759; et *Leo Afer*, edit. Lugdun. l. 2. 212, etc., and *Purchas* ex Leone, l. 2, tom 2, 795.' [3] Both these notes, according to Professor Hanford, are probably to be dated between 1639 and 1644.[4] These two accounts of Numidian poets deal with the practice and encouragement of poetry among the Arabs in northern Africa. Both descriptions are from the *Collections of things most remarkable in Iohn Leo his third Booke of the Historie of Africa*. The first passage is concise:

The greater part of *Arabians* which inhabite *Numidia*, are very witty and conceited in penning of verses; wherein each man will decypher his loue, his hunting, his combates, and other his worthy acts: and this is done for the most part in rime, after the *Italian* manner. . . . Those which possesse the Desarts bordering upon the Kingdomes of *Tremizen* and *Tunis* . . . take great delight in Poetrie, and will pen most excellent verses, their language being very pure and elegant. If any worthy Poet be found among them, he is accepted by their Gouernours with great honour and liberalitie; neither would any man easily belieue what wit and decencie is in their verses.[5]

The second account is more detailed:

In *Fez* there are diuers most excellent Poets, which make Verses in their owne Mother-tongue: most of their Poems and Songs intreate of Loue. Euery yeare they pen certaine Verses in the commendation of *Mahumet*, especially upon his Birth-day: for then betimes in the morning they resort unto the Palace of the chiefe Iudge or Gouernour, ascending his Tribunall seate, and from thence reading their Verses to a great audience of people: and he whose Verses are most elegant and pithy, is that yeare proclaimed Prince of the Poets. But when as the Kings of the *Marin* Family prospered, they vsed to inuite all the learned men of the Citie unto their Palace; and honourably entertaining them, they commanded each man in their hearing to recite their Verses to the commendation of *Mahumet*; and hee that was in all mens opinions esteemed the best Poet, was rewarded by the King with an hundred Duckats, with an excellent Horse, with a Woman-slaue, and with the Kings owne Robes wherewith hee was then apparelled: all the rest had fifty Duckats apiece giuen them, so that none departed without the Kings liberalitie; but an hundred and thirtie yeares are expired since this custome, together with the Maiestie of the *Fezzan* Kingdome decayed.[6]

Here, then, is proof positive that Milton read Purchas. Why may the poet not have derived some of his mythological details from Purchas' other popular book, the *Pilgrimage?* The passage from that book which describes the rites of Moloch has already been mentioned,[7] a passage which is linked to Milton by the word 'timbrels.' To be sure, exactly the same word occurs in Sandys' version of the same ghastly business,[8] but there are a number of parallels between Milton and Purchas, whereas the resemblance to Sandys seems to be isolated.

There is another instance of similarity in the matter of the goddess Ashtoreth, who appears in *Paradise Lost*, i, 438–446:

> . . . Astoreth, whom the Phoenicians called
> Astarte, queen of heaven, with crescent horns;
> To whose bright image nightly by the moon
> Sidonian virgins paid their vows and songs;
> In Sion also not unsung, where stood
> Her temple also on the offensive mountain, built
> By that uxorious king whose heart, though large,
> Beguiled by fair idolatresses, fell
> To idols foul.

Purchas says of her in the *Pilgrimage*,

Astarte or *Asteroth* was worshipped in the formes of sheepe, not of the Sydonians onely, but of the Philistims also. . . . And wise *Salomon* was brought by doting on women, to a worse dotage of idolatry with this Sydonian Idoll among others.[9]

The mention of Solomon in connection with Ashtoreth is inevitable from the account in 1 Kings 11.
Again Purchas says:

> The Sidonians also worshipped *Astarte*, in a stately
> and ancient Temple to her builded: whom some inter-
> pret *Luna*, some *Venus*. . . . *Luna* also after *Lucian*.
> And so it appeareth by her hornie head. . . . Shee ware
> on her head in stead of a Crowne a Bulleshead: whereby
> what else could be meant but the Moone Queene of the
> night? as the Sunne *Baalsamen* is King of Heauen or
> Lord of the day.[10]

Purchas, like Milton, treats Ashtoreth as a lunar
deity, and the phrase, 'the Moone Queene of the
night,' may even have been recalled in Milton's
'Astarte, queen of heaven.' This detail is ulti-
mately derived from Lucian, as Professor Cook
has pointed out: [11]

$$\text{'}A\sigma\tau\acute{a}\rho\tau\eta\nu \ \delta\text{' } \grave{\epsilon}\gamma\grave{\omega} \ \delta o\kappa\acute{\epsilon}\omega \ \Sigma\epsilon\lambda\eta\nu a\acute{\iota}\eta\nu \ \acute{\epsilon}\mu\mu\epsilon\nu a\iota.$$[12]

On the same page with the account of Ashtoreth
in Purchas is a description of the mourning for
Thammuz or Adonis, one person under two
names: [13]

> *Lucian* sayth, that he saw also at *Biblos* the Temple
> of *Venus Biblia*, wherein are celebrated the yeerely rites
> of *Adonis* . . . with beatings and wofull lamentings;
> after which, they perform Obsequies unto him, and

the next day they affirme him to be aliue, and shaue
their heads. And such women as will not be shauen,
must prostitute their bodies for one day vnto strangers,
and the money hence accrewing, is sacred to *Venus*. . . .
This is called the *mourning for Thamuz*. . . . Women
were the chiefe lomenters, if not the onely, as *Ezechiel*
testifieth. . . . Hereby (i.e. by Biblos) runneth the
Riuer Adonis also, which once a yeere becommeth red
and bloudie: which alteration of the colour of the water,
is the warning . . . that their *Mourning for Adonis*, who
at that time they say is wounded in Libanus: whereas
that rednesse ariseth indeed of the winds, which, at that
time blowing violently, doe with their force carry downe
alongst the streame a great quantity of that red Earth
or *Minium* of Libanus whereby it passeth.[14]

Milton's version is very similar (*Paradise Lost*, i,
446–457):

> Thammuz came next behind,
> Whose annual wound in Lebanon allured
> The Syrian damsels to lament his fate
> In amorous ditties all a summer's day,
> While smooth Adonis from his native rock
> Ran purple to the sea, supposed with blood
> Of Thammuz yearly wounded: the love-tale
> Infected Sion's daughters with like heat,
> Whose wanton passions in the sacred porch
> Ezekiel saw, when, by the vision led,
> His eye surveyed the dark idolatries
> Of alienated Judah.

The description by Purchas repeats substantially Lucian's account of the same event,[15] which Milton must certainly have known, whether late or early in his career. Is it a wild flight of imagination to suppose that Milton might have read Purchas before he read Lucian, and so had the story imprinted on his memory in an English rather than a Greek form? I do not know at what age an English schoolboy of Milton's day would have been likely to read Lucian, but it seems probable that as popular a book as *Purchas his Pilgrimage* would have found its way within a few years of publication into as cultured a household as that of the elder Milton. The book appeared in 1617, when Milton was nine years old. We have no more direct evidence on the case than that Milton was taking notes on the *Pilgrimes* fairly well along in the history of the *Commonplace Book*, probably between 1639 and 1644,[16] but that does not mean that he may not have done his initial reading in Purchas while he was still a schoolboy and possibly before he knew Lucian. However that may be, there are certainly striking points of likeness between the two descriptions of the lamentation for Thammuz.

There is one detail in the description of Typhon by both Milton and Purchas which might strengthen the case for a connection between them. Milton, in his *Nativity Ode*, l. 226, speaks of

> Typhon huge, ending in snaky twine,

while Purchas says, 'His legges were entwined with rolls of Vipers.' [17] This may be only a stock description, but 'twine' and 'entwined' are close enough to look like a recollection.

Since Purchas is only a compiler of other people's results, one can nowhere say that Milton must have drawn any given detail from him and from no one else. But the indubitable resemblances between the two suggest an interesting study, to determine whether Milton really did owe something to Purchas, or whether they were both repeating commonplaces.

D

The Authorized Version translates Azazel in Leviticus, 16, 8, as 'scapegoat,' which hardly seems appropriate as the name of an angel, but such is the meaning assigned to that of the cherub Azazel by many of the commentators. Callander, however, recognized the name as belonging to one of the twenty leaders of the fallen angels given in the Syncellus fragment of the *Book of Enoch*.[1] Azazel appears again, in the next chapter of *Enoch*, as the artificer-angel, who, after the fall of the angels, instructed men in arts and crafts.[2] Callander says, in his note on this subject:[3]

This is the name of one of the Ἐγρήγοροι, or Angels, who, according to the Jewish tradition, fell in love with the daughters of men before the flood, and having polluted themselves with them, were cast out of heaven by God, as a punishment of their crime. The author of the fragment under the name of the Patriarch Enoch, calls one of their chiefs Azalzel, Ἀζαλζελ.

This discovery in 1750 antedates the recent work done on the same point by Professor Saurat,

but the French professor goes more thoroughly
into the subject, as well as into the general connection between Milton and the *Book of Enoch*.[4]
These are striking parallels that Professor Saurat
brings out: the motive of sensuality in Milton's
account of Satan's first succumbing to sin in
Heaven, *Paradise Lost*, ii, 761–767, and in the fall
of the angels in the Judaic tradition represented
by *Enoch*;[5] the description of the warfare between
men and giants, who are, in *Enoch*, the offspring
of the fallen angels;[6] the cultivation of the arts by
men who, in *Enoch*, are instructed by the lost
angels;[7] and the names of the four faithful angels,
Michael, Gabriel, Uriel, and Raphael, who, in
Enoch, represented the tale of the griefs of men to
God.[8]

All these points were in the fragment of *Enoch*
retained by Georgius Syncellus, the Byzantine
chronicler of the eighth century, in his *Chronog-
raphy from Adam to Diocletian*, which was published in Paris in 1652.[9] This fragment was the
only part of the *Book of Enoch* available in Milton's
lifetime. Professor Saurat points this out, without,
however, mentioning the fact that since Milton
went blind in the same year as the publication of

Syncellus' book, it would have had to be read aloud to him. If Milton knew Syncellus in this way, as seems probable from the closeness of the parallels cited by Professor Saurat, this would be an interesting example of a book that Milton knew well enough to draw on for much material, without ever having seen one of its pages.

E

1. Its Curriculum according to the *Statutes*

As towchyng in this scole what shalbe taught
of the Maisters and lernyd of the scolers it passith
my wit to devyse and determyn in particuler but
in generall to speke and sum what to saye my
mynde, I wolde they were taught all way in good
litterature both laten and greke, and goode auctors
suych as haue the veray Romayne eliquence joyned
withe wisdome specially Cristyn auctours that
wrote theyre wysdome with clene and chast laten
other in verse or in prose, for my entent is by thys
scole specially to incresse knowlege and worship-
ping of god and oure lorde Crist Jesu and good
Cristen lyff and maners in the Children And for
that entent I will the Chyldren lerne ffirst aboue
all the Cathechyzon in Englysh and after the
accidence that I made or sum other yf eny be
better to the purpose to induce chyldren more
spedely to laten spech And thanne Institutum
Christiani homines [1] which that lernyd Erasmus

made at my request and the boke Copia of the
same Erasmus And thenne other auctours Christian as lactancius prudentius and proba and sedulius and Juuencus and Baptista Mantuanus and
suche other as shalbe tought convenyent and
moste to purpose vnto the true laten spech all
barbary all corrupcion all laten adulerate which
ignorant blynde folis brought into this worlde and
with the same hath distayned and poysenyd the
olde laten spech and the varay Romayne tong
which in the tyme of Tully and Salust and Virgill
and Terence was usid, whiche also seint Jerome
and seint ambrose and seint Austen and many
hooly doctors lernyd in theyr tymes. I say that
ffylthynesse and all such abusyon which the later
blynde worlde brought in which more ratheyr may
be callid blotterature thenne litterature I vtterly
abbanysh and Exclude oute of this scole and
charge the Maisters that they teche all way that
is the best and instruct the chyldren in greke and
Redyng laten in Redyng vnto them suych auctours
that hathe with wisdome joyned the pure chaste
eloquence.[2]

2. Influence of the Prayers

There is nothing new in saying that a school
with the antiquity and the traditions of St. Paul's
must have had a profound influence on the mind
of a sensitive boy like John Milton. Commentators
have dwelt [3] on the beauty of his memories of 'the
studious cloister's pale,' and on the love he shows
in his poems for churchly architecture and pealing
organ music,[4] which was part of the heritage of
a schoolboy who lived under the majestic shadow
of St. Paul's Cathedral. But it has not been
pointed out that the very prayers that he heard
repeated in weekly rotation must have had their
effect on his memory as well.

Since the school was dedicated from the outset
to the Boy Jesus,[5] the whole religious thought of
the place centred about the outstanding episode
of His boyhood, the teaching in the temple. 'Over
the high master's chair is a beautifully-wrought
figure of the Child Jesus, seated, in the attitude of
one teaching; and all the young flock, as they
enter and leave school, salute it with a hymn'; so.
wrote Erasmus to Justus Jonas in 1519,[6] and the
probabilities are that veneration for tradition

would have preserved such a custom until Milton's time. It is certain that the reading of Latin prayers still survives.[7] Two of the prayers appointed for the afternoon or evening use of the school emphasize the same idea of the Boy Jesus as teacher, in Latin phraseology that must, from numberless repetitions, have impressed itself indelibly on Milton's boyish mind. The first is the beautiful prayer for use on Monday afternoons:

Oratiuncula ad puerum Iesum, Scholae Praesidem

Capellanus. Domine noster, Iesu suavissime, qui puer adhuc anno aetatis tuae duodecimo in Hierosolymitano templo inter doctores illos sic disputasti, ut stupefacti universi tuam super excellentem sapientiam admirarentur, te quaesumus ut in hac tua Schola, cui praes et patrocinaris, eam quotidie discamus et literaturam et sapientiam, qua possimus in primis te, Iesu, qui es vera sapientia, cognoscere, deinde cognitum eundem te colere et imitari; atque in hac brevi vita sic ambulare in via doctrinae tuae, sequaces vestigiorum tuorum, ut, quo pervenisti ipse, ad aliquam ejus gloriae partem, decendentes ex hac luce, possimus nos quoque tua gratia feliciter pervenire.

Chorus. Amen.[8]

The second prayer, which is still used in the school,[9] was appointed to be read on Wednesday afternoons:

Capellanus. Precamur, Iesu Christe, ut qui puer duodecim annos natus, sedens in templo, docuisti ipsos doctores, cuique Pater caelitus emissa voce dedit auctoritatem docendi mortalium genus, quum diceret: HIC EST FILIUS MEUS DILECTUS, IN QUO MIHI COMPLACITUM EST: IPSUM AUDITE; quique es aeterna sapientia summi Patris; illustrare digneris ingenia nostra ad perdiscendas honestas literas, quibus utamur ad tuam gloriam; qui vivis et regnas, cum Patre et Spiritu Sancto, semper unus Deus in saecula saeculorum.

Chorus. Amen.[10]

There is no single detail of the boyhood of Jesus in these prayers that is not taken from the second chapter of Luke. The same details are used in Milton's account (*Paradise Regained*, i, 201–214):

> When I was yet a child, no childish play
> To me was pleasing; all my mind was set
> Serious to learn and know, and thence to do,
> What might be public good; myself I thought
> Born to that end, born to promote all truth,
> All righteous things. Therefore, above my years,
> The Law of God I read, and found it sweet;
> Made it my whole delight, and in it grew
> To such perfection that, ere yet my age
> Had measured twice six years, at our great Feast
> I went into the Temple, there to hear
> The teachers of our Law, and to propose
> What might improve my knowledge or their own,
> And was admired by all.

What Milton himself adds shows that he had brooded over his conception of the youth of Christ until he could supplement the brief Biblical story by the force of his own imagination. This is a serious Puritan child that he portrays, who knew no more about play than we can imagine Milton's knowing as a boy. Whence came this conception? Partly from his own studious youth, partly from the Bible, partly from the religious teachings of his school — and who can tell in what proportions?

There is, then, no textual proof that the prayers of his school days contributed any detail exclusively their own to the picture in *Paradise Regained*. But the fact remains that this portion of the story of the life of Christ must have become, during his boyhood, a part of the very grain of his consciousness, and these details must have risen unbidden in his mind, when, as a man of sixty, he came to write of the Boy Christ in *Paradise Regained*.

NOTES

NOTES

I

1. J. Milton, *De Doctrina Christiana* (ed. C. R. Sumner, Cambridge, 1825), p. 5. 'De me, libris tantummodo sacris adhaeresco; haeresin aliam, sectam aliam sequor nullam.'
2. *Milton's Prose Works* (ed. Bohn, London, 1853), iii, 118.
3. *Prose Works*, ii, 388.
4. William Laud, Archbishop of Canterbury, *Works* (6th ed., Oxford, 1849), ii, vol. in *Library of Anglo-Catholic Theology*.
5. *Ibid.*, 'Editor's Preface,' p. xviii. '"Fisher the Jesuit" . . . was only a name assumed by a person named Piersey, Piers, Percy, or Persy . . . of whom . . . facts are recorded in the Bibliotheca Scriptorum Societatis Jesu (ed. Alegambe et Sotwell, Romae, 1676) — in Dodd's Ch. History — and in H. More (Hist. Soc. Jesu).'
6. From Laud's diary. *Ibid.*, p. xi.
7. *Ibid.*, p. ix.
8. *Ibid.*, p. 387. Only one citation, usually the first, is given from each Father.
9. *Ibid.*, p. 379.
10. *Ibid.*, p. 25.
11. *Ibid.*, p. 387.
12. *Ibid.*, p. 138.

13. *Ibid.*, pp. 5–8.
14. *Ibid.*, p. 13.
15. *Ibid.*, pp. 205–206.
16. *Ibid.*, p. 12.
17. *Ibid.*, pp. 389–390.
18. *Ibid.*, p. 33.
19. *Ibid.*, pp. 9–12.
20. *Ibid.*, p. 388.
21. *Ibid.*, p. 386.
22. *Ibid.*, p. 310.
23. *Ibid.*, p. 61, note q.
24. *Ibid.*, p. 2, note c.
25. *Ibid.*, p. 88, note i.
26. *Ibid.*, p. 90, note m.
27. *Prose Works*, i, 38, 62, 69, 71, 74, 79–82, 102, 104, 106–107; *Ibid.*, pp. 437–439.
28. *Ibid.*, ii, 384.
29. *Ibid.*, p. 379.
30. P. Pritchard, *The Influence of the Fathers upon Milton, with Especial Reference to Augustine* (Cornell University, 1925).
31. *Prose Works*, ii, 426–427.
32. *Ibid.*, p. 426.
33. *Ibid.*, p. 428.
34. *Ibid.*, p. 427.
35. *Ibid.*, p. 378.
36. *An Humble Remonstrance to the High Court of Parliament, by a dutifull Sonne of the Church* (London, 1641), pp. 41–42. 'Is it a Title, or a Retinue, or a Ceremony, a garment, or a colour, or an Organpipe, that can make us a different Church, whiles we

preach and professe the same saving Truth? . . . We
are all your true brethren; we are one with you,
both in heart and brain; and hope to meet you in
the same heaven.'

37. *Prose Works*, ii, 375.
38. *Ibid.*, p. 399.
39. *Of Reformation* (ed. W. T. Hale, New Haven: Yale
University Press, 1916), Yale Studies in English,
liv, p. xxxv.
40. *Prose Works*, ii, 380.
41. *Ibid.*, pp. 481–482.
42. P. Pritchard, *op. cit.*, pp. 5–6.
43. *Prose Works*, ii, 422.
44. *Ibid.*, p. 435.
45. *Ibid.*, p. 548.
46. *Ibid.*, iii, 163.
47. *Ibid.*, p. 66.
48. *Ibid.*, p. 415.
49. *Ibid.*, p. 416.
50. *Ibid.*, p. 421.
51. *Ibid.*, p. 423.
52. *Ibid.*, ii, 435.
53. P. Pritchard, *op. cit.*, p. 5.
54. *Prose Works*, ii, 375.
55. P. Pritchard, *op. cit.*, p. 31.
56. *Encyclopædia Britannica* (11th ed., Cambridge,
1910), xiv, 292.
57. J. P. Migne, *Patrologiae Graecae* (Paris, 1857), v,
386, πρέπον ἐστὶν ὑμῖν, ὡς Ἐκκλησία Θεοῦ, χειροτονῆσαι
ἐπίσκοπον εἰς τὸ πρεσβεῦσαι ἐκεῖ Θεοῦ πρεσβείαν, etc.
58. *Ibid.*, p. 705.

59. J. H. Hanford, 'The Chronology of Milton's Private Studies,' *Publications of the Modern Language Association*, xxxvi (1921), 264, n. 28.
60. L. Pautigny, 'Justin. Apologies,' *Textes et documents pour l'étude historique du christianisme* (Paris, 1904), p. x.
61. O. Bardenhewer, *Geschichte der Altkirchlichen Literatur* (2d ed., Freiburg, 1913), i, 215.
62. J. H. Hanford, *op. cit.*, p. 265, n. 29a.

II

1. *A Commonplace Book of John Milton* (ed. A. J. Horwood, Camden Society, 1876), pp. 1, 3, 4, 21, 50 (pp. 4, 5, 14, 18, 178, 241 of Milton's paging).
2. *Prose Works*, ii, 385; iii, 417.
3. *Ibid.*, ii, 389.
4. D. Masson, *The Life of John Milton* (London: Macmillan, 1894), ii, 253.
5. *The Whole Works of the Most Reverend James Usher*, *D.D.* (Dublin, 1847), vii, 75–85.
6. J. H. Hanford, *op. cit.*, pp. 260–261.
7. Milton's and Usher's patristic citations:

*Commonplace Book**	*Judgment of Dr. Rainoldes*
TERTULLIAN	
P. 4, *De Spectaculis* (ed. Rigalt), p. 102.	P. 81, note e ⎫ *De Praescriptionibus adversus Haereticos*, chap. 32.
P. 241, *De Spectaculis* (ed. Rigalt), no page given.	P. 83, note q ⎭
P. 13, *De Jejuniis* (ed. Rigalt), p. 703.	P. 81, note e ⎱ *Contra Marcionem*, Bk. IV, chap. 5.
P. 181, *Apologeticus* (ed. Rigalt), p. 31.	P. 83, note r ⎰

* Milton's paging.

NOTES 173

IGNATIUS

P. 109, *Epistola ad Philadelphenses*, pp. 94–95.

P. 79, notes p, q, r, s, t, *Epistola ad Ephesios.*

P. 79, notes u, x, y, *Epistola ad Smyrnaeos.*

CLEMENT OF ALEXANDRIA

P. 71, *Stromata*, vii, 730.
P. 106, *Paedagogos*, ii, c. 2, 158.
P. 109, *Stromata*, iii, 448.

Pp. 84–85, note z, *Liber de divite salvando.*

8. See pp. 65–66.
9. P. Pritchard, *op. cit.*, pp. 11–12.
10. *Commonplace Book*, p. 1. The italicized words are a direct quotation from Tertullian. See *Tertullianus* (ed. F. Oehler, Leipzig, 1853), i, 59. 'In malo morali potest multum esse admistum boni, idque arte singulari; *nemo venenum temperat felle et helleboro sed conditis pulmentis et bene saporatis: ita diabolus letale quod conficit rebus dei gratissimis imbuit,* etc. *Tertull:* de spectaculis, p. 102, edit. Rigalt.'
11. Rome: Conrad Sweynheym and Arnold Panartz, 1470
    Venice: Wendelin of Speier, 1472
    Rome: Chardella, 1474
    Venice: Johann of Cologne and Johann Manthen, 1478
             Andreas de Paltasichis and Boninus de Boninis, 1479
             Theodorus de Ragazonibus, 1490
             Vincentius Benalius, 1493
             Bonetus Locatellus, 1494
             Joannes Tacuinus de Tridino, 1502

Florence: Iuntina, 1513
Venice: Aldus Manutius, 1515; 1535
Basle: Cratandrus, 1521; 1524
Cologne: Gymnicus, 1539; 1555
Lyons: Tornaesius and Gazeius, 1556
Leyden: Thysius, 1652
         Gallaeus, 1660

12. J. H. Hanford, *op. cit.*, p. 258.

13. See n. 10 above.

14. J. H. Hanford, *op. cit.*, p. 265.

15. *Ibid.*, pp. 264 n. 29, 265. For further adoption of the Italian style of handwriting, see E. K. Rand, '"J" and "I" in Milton's Latin Script,' *Modern Philology*, xix (1922), 315–319.

16. J. H. Hanford, *op. cit.*, pp. 255–256.

17. See Appendix A, 1.

18. See Appendix A, 2.

19. *The Works of Lactantius* (trans. W. Fletcher), ii, 28, *Ante-Nicene Christian Library* (ed. A. Roberts and J. Donaldson, Edinburgh, 1871). The exact passage is *De Ira Dei*, chap. 13, § 20.

20. See Appendix A, 1.

21. *Divinae Institutiones, Corpus Scriptorum Ecclesiasticorum Latinorum* (ed. Samuel Brandt, Vienna, 1893), vol. xix, Bk. III, chap. 29, § 16, p. 270.

22. *Ibid.*, Bk. II, chap. 17, § 1, p. 172.
    III, chap. 29, §§ 16–20, pp. 270–271.
    V, chap. 7, §§ 3–10, pp. 419–421.
    chap. 22, §§ 2–5, 17, pp. 473, 476.
    VI, chap. 4, § 17, p. 493.
    chap. 15, §§ 5–7, 9, pp. 537–538.

        chap. 20, § 3, p. 556.
        chap. 22, § 2, p. 564.
    VII, chap. 4, §§ 12–14, p. 595.
        chap. 5, §§ 9, 24, pp. 597–598, 601.
  Epitome, *CSEL*, vol. xix, chap. 24, pp. 697–699.
        chap. 29, § 7, p. 705.

23. *Prose Works*, ii, 67. 'Good and evil we know in the field of this world grow up together almost inseparably; and the knowledge of good is so involved and interwoven with the knowledge of evil, and in so many cunning resemblances hardly to be discerned, that those confused seeds, which were imposed upon Psyche as an incessant labour to cull out, and sort asunder, were not more intermixed.'

    Ibid., p. 68. 'As therefore the state of man now is; what wisdom can there be to choose, what continence to forbear, without the knowledge of evil? He that can apprehend and consider vice with all her baits and seeming pleasures, and yet abstain, and yet distinguish, and yet prefer that which is truly better, he is the true warfaring Christian.'

    Ibid., p. 74. 'If every action which is good or evil in man at ripe years, were to be under pittance, prescription, and compulsion, what were virtue but a name, what praise could be then due to well doing, what gramercy to be sober, just, or continent?'

    Ibid., p. 75. 'Suppose we could expel sin by this means; look how much we thus expel of sin, so

much we expel of virtue: for the matter of them
both is the same: remove that, and ye remove
them both alike.'

24. *Div. Insts.*, Bk. III, chap. 29, § 16, p. 270. 'idcirco
enim in primordiis transgressionis non statim ad
poenam detrusus a deo est, ut hominem malitia
sua *exerceat* ad uirtutem.'

Ibid., Bk. V, chap. 7, §4, p. 419. 'nunc designare
id breuissime satis est, uirtutem aut cerni non
posse, nisi habeat uitia contraria, aut non esse
perfectam, nisi *exerceatur* aduersis.'

Ibid., Bk. VII, chap. 4, § 13, p. 595. 'idcirco enim
data est illi sapientia, ut cognita bonorum malo-
rumque natura et in adpetendis bonis et in malis
declinandis uim suae rationis *exerceat.*'

25. See p. 21.

26. *Prose Works*, ii, 68.

27. *Div. Insts.*, Bk. III, chap. 29, § 16, p. 270. 'ex quo
fit ut uirtus nulla sit, si *aduersarius* desit.'

Ibid., §§ 19, 20, p. 271. 'sed ut *aduersarium* suum
nesciunt, sic ne uirtutem quidem sciunt, cuius
scientia ab *aduersarii* notione descendit. . . . nemo
enim potest ueris armis instrui, si hostem contra
quem fuerit armandus ignorat, nec *aduersarium*
uincere qui in dimicando non hostem uerum, sed
umbram petit.'

Ibid., Bk. V, chap. 22, § 17, p. 476. 'quomodo enim
potest imperator militum suorum probare uirtutem, nisi habuerit hostem? et illi tamen *aduersarius* exsurgit inuito, quia mortalis est et uinci
potest, deo autem quia repugnari non potest, ipse

aduersarios nomini suo excitat, non qui contra
ipsum deum pugnent, sed contra milites eius, ut
deuotionem ac fidem suorum uel probet uel con-
roboret, donec pressurae uerberibus diffluentem
corrigat disciplinam.'

Ibid., Bk. VI, chap. 4, § 17, p. 493. 'sic in omni
hac uita, quia nobis *aduersarium* deus reseruauit,
ut possemus capere uirtutem, omittenda est prae-
sens uoluptas, ne hostis opprimat, uigilandum,
stationes agendae, militares expeditiones obeun-
dae, fundendus ad ultimum cruor, omnia denique
amara et grauia patienter ferenda, eo quidem
promptius, quod nobis imperator noster deus
praemia pro laboribus aeterna constituit.'

Ibid., chap. 15, § 7, p. 537. 'ubi ergo uitia non sunt,
ne uirtuti quidem locus est, sicut ne uictoriae
quidem, ubi *aduersarius* nullus est. ita fit ut
bonum sine malo esse in hac uita non possit.'

28. *Ibid.*, Bk. III, chap. 29, § 16, p. 270.

29. *Ibid.*, § 19, p. 271.

30. *L. Annaei Senecae Dialogorum Liber I* (ed. Emil
Hermes, Leipzig: Teubner, 1905), *De Providentia*,
chap. 2, § 2, p. 3. 'omnia adversa *exercitationes*
putat.'

Ibid., § 4, p. 3. 'marcet sine *adversario* virtus.'

Ibid., § 7, p. 4. 'miraris tu, si deus ille bonorum
amantissimus, qui illos quam optimos esse atque
excellentissimos vult, fortunam illis cum qua
exerceantur adsignat?'

31. *CSEL*, XXVII, ii, 2, 263.

32. *Prose Works*, ii, 68.

33. *Commonplace Book*, p. 1 (p. 5 of Milton's paging).
34. J. H. Hanford, *op. cit.*, p. 279, n. 141.
35. *Ibid.*, p. 285.
36. See Appendix A, 3.
37. *Commonplace Book*, p. 3 (p. 14 of Milton's paging).
38. *Div. Insts.*, Bk. VI, chap. 23, § 9, p. 566.
39. *Commonplace Book*, p. 3 (p. 14 of Milton's paging).
40. J. H. Hanford, *op. cit.*, p. 265.
41. Geoffrey of Monmouth, *Historiae Regum Britanniae*, ii, 6. 'Relicta quoque propria uxore sua, ex qua inclytum juvenem Ebraucum genuerat, sese Sodomitanae libidini dedidit non naturalem Venerem naturali voluptati praeferens.'
42. *Prose Works*, v, 174.
43. *Commonplace Book*, p. 4 (p. 18 of Milton's paging).
44. J. H. Hanford, *op. cit.*, p. 271, n. 67; p. 279, n. 135.
45. See Appendix A, 4.
46. Lucretius, *De Rerum Natura*, v, 223 ff.
47. *Commonplace Book*, p. 21 (p. 178 of Milton's paging).
48. See Appendix A, 5.
49. J. H. Hanford, *op. cit.*, p. 267.
50. *Commonplace Book*, p. 50 (p. 241 of Milton's paging).
51. *Ibid.*, p. 50. '*Tertullianus*, in eo libro quem de spectaculis inscripsit, damnat eorum usum, et Christianis occludit, nec vero tantum argumentis agit (quae solos ethnicos ludos convellunt) ut cauti et prudentis Christiani animum religione obstringere debuerit, quo minus poema aliquod dramaticum a poetâ non imperito concinnatum spectare

ausit; illud tamen optime facit in epilogo libri ut
mentem Christiani ad meliora h.e. divina et celestia
spectacula (quae tot et tanta homo Christianus
animo praecipere potest [printed *protest*]) de adventu
Christi, de futuro judicio, densis coloribus contortis
incitaverit. eundem prorsus lapidem volvit *Cypria-
nus* seu quis alius libro eâdem de re composito
tom. 3.'

52. *Tertullianus, De Spectaculis* (ed. F. Oehler, Leipzig,
1853), vol. i, chap. 30, p. 61. 'Quale autem spec-
taculum in proximo est adventus domini iam indu-
bitati, iam superbi, iam triumphantis! quae illa
exultatio angelorum, quae gloria resurgentium sanc-
torum! quale regnum exinde iustorum! qualis
civitas nova Hierusalem! At enim supersunt alia
spectacula, ille ultimus et perpetuus iudicii dies,
ille nationibus insperatus, ille derisus, cum tanta
saeculi vetustas, et tot eius nativitates uno igni
haurientur.'

53. *Prose Works*, ii, 388.

54. *Ibid.*, iii, 155.

55. See n. 52 above.

56. René Pichon, *Lactance, étude sur le mouvement philosophique et religieux sous le règne de Constantin*
(Paris, 1901), p. 181.

57. *Ibid.*, p. 182.

58. *Ibid.*, p. 307. See also pp. 266–334.

59. *Ibid.*, pp. 1–2. 'Les Africains sont en général doués
d'une forte individualité qu'ils ne craignent pas
d'étaler dans leurs oeuvres: Lactance met dans la
sienne très peu de lui-même; son tempérament s'y

révèle à peine; il ne nous fait aucune confidence;
l'impersonnalité des *Institutions Divines* contraste
avec le "moi" exubérant de Tertullien. . . . Les
Africains, violents et extrêmes, vont jusqu'au bout
de leurs idées et surtout de leurs passions, qui les
dominent bien plus que leurs idées: Lactance est
l'homme du juste milieu, dût-il paraître un peu
froid, un peu trop purement rationnel. Les Africains dédaignent la tradition littéraire pour la mo-
dernité la plus aiguë: Lactance est le plus fervent
admirateur de Cicéron, son imitateur le plus fidèle.
Le style africain, obsédé par la sensation vive et
brusque, est fait de rapidité et de pittoresque avant
tout: le style de Lactance est périodique, oratoire
et abstrait. . . . L'exemple de Lactance est un des
meilleurs arguments contre la théorie de la race et
du climat.'

60. See Appendix A, 6.
61. *Div. Insts.*, Bk. VI, chap. 21, § 11, p. 563. 'cuius
    terminos si quis excesserit nihilque aliut ex uolup-
    tate petierit nisi ipsam uoluptatem, hic mortem
    meditatur, quia sicut uita perpetua in uirtute est,
    ita mors in uoluptate.'
62. See Appendix A, 7.
63. *Milton's Poetical Works* (ed. D. Masson, London,
    1890), ii, 587.

III

1. *The Poetical Works of John Milton* (London, 1695),
   'Annotations on Milton's *Paradise Lost* by P. H.
   Φιλοποιήτης.'
2. *Ibid.*, p. 6, Bk. I, l. 46.

3. *Ibid.*, p. 24, l. 406.
4. *Ibid.*, p. 4, l. 17.
5. *Ibid.*, p. 24, .l 395.
6. *Ibid.*, p. 4, l. 21.
7. *Ibid.*, p. 6, l. 46.
8. *Ibid.*, p. 1.
9. *Ibid.*
10. *Ibid.*, p. 4, Bk. I, l. 17.
11. Hesiod, *Theogony*, 132–138.

αὐτὰρ ἔπειτα
Οὐρανῷ εὐνηθεῖσα, τέκ' Ὠκεανὸν βαθυδίνην,
Κοῖόν τε, Κρεῖόν θ', Ὑπερίονά τ', Ἰαπετόν τε,
Θείάν τε, Ῥείαν τε, Θέμιν τε, Μνημοσύνην τε,
Φοίβην τε χρυσοστέφανον, Τηθύν τ' ἐρατεινήν.
τοὺς δὲ μέθ' ὁπλότατος γένετο Κρόνος ἀγκυλομήτης,
δεινότατος παίδων· θαλερὸν δ' ἤχθηρε τοκῆα·

12. *P. L.* (ed. T. Keightley, London, 1859), i, 232. 'We may observe that there is no such person as Titan in Grecian mythology. The twelve Titans were Heaven's first-born, and it was Heaven who was deprived of his power by his son, Kronos or Saturn.'

P. L., Bk. I (ed. E. F. Willoughby, in Maynard's English Classic Series, London, 1879), p. 72. 'Milton's mythology is here a little wrong: there was no individual Titan; the Titans, according to Hesiod, were the six sons and six daughters of Ouranos (Heaven) and Gaia (Earth), among whom were Kronos and Rhea.'

Milton, *Poetical Works* (ed. D. Masson, London, 1890), iii, 397. 'Titan is named as the earliest supreme god; superseded by Saturn; who, in his turn, is dethroned by Zeus.' Masson himself, although he does not accuse Milton of false scholarship, does not speak as if he recognized the source of Milton's usage.

P. L., Bks. I–II (ed. A. W. Verity, Cambridge, 1893), p. 96. 'Apparently M. thinks that there was some individual deity called Titan, and that he, not Uranus, was the father of the twelve Titans: what authority — if any — he had for this view I know not.'

P. L., Bks. I–II (ed. H. B. Sprague, Boston, 1898), p. 43. 'This was Oceanus, eldest of the twelve Titans, and by his birth entitled to succeed his father, Uranus, on the throne? He is called "Titan" *par excellence* by Lactantius and by Milton, just as "the mightiest Julius" is especially styled "Caesar."' The curious part of this note is that, in spite of having cited the account in Lactantius, the editor persists in the idea that Titan must perforce be the eldest of the twelve Titans.

P. L., Bks. I–IV (ed. J. L. Robertson, in Blackwood's English Classics, Edinburgh, 1900), p. 126. 'Titan was the family name; no individual member appropriated it; and it was Uranus whom Saturn deposed, not one of his brothers.'

C. G. Osgood, *The Classical Mythology of Milton's English Poems*, Yale Studies in English, viii (New York: Henry Holt, 1900), 82. 'Titan . . . Milton speaks of Oceanus as the first-born, and as afterward deprived of his birthright by the younger Saturn (Cronus).'

P. L., Bks. I–II (ed. H. C. Beeching, in Clarendon Press Series, Oxford, 1901), p. 103. 'This is a mistake. The Titans were sons, not of *Titan*, which is not a proper name, but of Uranus.'

13. See Appendix B.

14. Boccaccio, *Genealogiae Deorum* (Paris, 1511), fol. xxix, Bk. IV, chap. 1.

15. *Recuyell of the Historyes of Troye* (trans. W. Caxton, London, 1894), i, 9–15, 18–33, 60–78.

16. Boccaccio, *op. cit.*, fol. xxix. 'Haec Lactantius ex historia sacra quae quam vera sint quasi eadem referens edocet Sybilla Erithrea.'

17. W. Caxton, *op. cit.*, i, 20, 33, 39, 50, 60, 215, 246, 271, 284.

18. R. Bentley, *Works* (ed. A. Dyce, London, 1836), ii, 256, 301, 330–331, 357.

19. R. Bentley, *Proposals for Printing a New Edition of the Greek Testament* (1720), p. 4.

20. R. C. Jebb, *Bentley*, in English Men of Letters Series (London, 1901), p. 162. 'Speaking generally of the work exhibited by the folio, we may say that its leading characteristics are two — wealth of patristic citation, and laborious attention to the order of words.'

21. R. Bentley, *Works*, ii, 103.

22. *Ibid.*, i, 172, 186, 291.

23. *P. L.*, Bk. I (ed. J. Callander, Glasgow, 1750), p. 10, l. 36.

24. *Ibid.*, p. 50, l. 341.

25. *Ibid.*, p. 70, l. 412.

26. *Ibid.*, p. 111, l. 534.

27. *Ibid.*, p. 10, l. 37.

28. *Ibid.*, p. 56, l. 375.

29. *Ibid.*, p. 70, l. 412.

30. *Ibid.*, p. 62.

31. G. Sandys, *A Relation of a Journey begun An. Dom. 1610* (London, 1615), p. 186 (quoted by Thomas Warton in *Milton's Poems upon Several Occasions*, ed. T. Warton, London, 1785, p. 282). 'Wherein (*i.e.*, in the valley of Tophet) the *Hebrews* sacrificed their children to *Molech*, an Idoll of brasse, hauing the head of a calfe, the rest of a kingly figure with armes extended to receiue the miserable sacrifice, seared to death with his burning embracements. For the Idoll was hollow within, and filled with fire. And lest their miserable shreeks should sad the hearts of their parents, the priests of *Molech* did deafe their eares with the continuall clangs of trumpets and timbrels.'

32. *Purchas his Pilgrimage* (London, 1617), Bk. I, chap. 18, p. 99. 'It was a hollow Image (saith *Lyra*) of Copper, in forme of a man. In the hollow concauitie was made a fire, with which the Idoll being heated, they put a childe into his armes, and the Priests made such a noyse with their Timbrels, that the cries of the childe might not moue the parents to compassion, but they should rather think the childes soule receiued of the god into rest and peace.'

For other references to a possible influence of Purchas on Milton, see Appendix C.

33. Callander, *op. cit.*, p. 75.

34. 2 Corinthians 11, 14.

35. *Div. Insts.*, Bk. II, chap. 14, §§ 13–14, p. 165.

36. *Ibid.*, §§ 11–12, p. 164.

37. Callander, *op. cit.*, p. 93.

38. Jerome, *Opera* (Cologne, 1616), v, 46; 'In Osee,' cap. IV. 'Videtur autem mihi iccirco et populus Israel in solitudine fecisse sibi caput vituli, quod coleret, et Hieroboam filius Nabath vitulos aureos fabricatus: ut quod in Aegypto didicerant ἄπιν καὶ μνεῦιν, qui sub figura boum coluntur, esse deos, hoc in sua superstitione seruarent.'

39. *Div. Insts.*, Bk. IV, chap. 10, §§ 11–12, p. 303.

40. Callander, *op. cit.*, p. 99.

41. *Div. Insts.*, Bk. I, chap. 5, § 7, p. 14.

42. *Ibid.*, chap. 11, § 55, p. 46.

43. *Ibid.*, §§ 52–53, p. 46. 'sed cum eadem ratione natum esse cogito, non possum putare deum summum quo uideam esse aliquid antiquius, caelum scilicet atque terram. . . . Saturnus autem si ex his natus est ut putatur, quemadmodum potest deus esse principalis qui aliis ortum suum debet aut quis praefuit mundo, priusquam Saturnus gigneretur?'

44. *Ibid.*, § 61, p. 47.

45. Callander, *op. cit.*, p. 100.

46. *Div. Insts.*, Bk. I, chap. 11, §§ 30–32, p. 41.

47. *Iliad*, Bk. XV, 189–192.

48. Callander, *op. cit.*, p. 101.

49. *Div. Insts.*, Bk. I, chap. 10, § 10, p. 35.

50. *Ibid.* chap. 11, §§ 45–46, p. 44.

51. Callander, *op. cit.*, p. 102. The passage is *Div. Insts.*, Bk. I, chap. 11, § 47, p. 45.

52. Callander, *op. cit.*, p. 138.

53. D. Saurat, *La pensée de Milton* (Paris: Félix Alcan, 1920), pp. 236 ff.

54. See p. 159.

55. *Div. Insts.*, Bk. II, chap. 14, §§ 1–5, pp. 162–163. *Epitome diuinarum institutionum*, chap. 22 (27), §§ 9–11, p. 695.

56. D. Saurat, *op. cit.*, p. 260. Professor Saurat quotes Canon Bareille, *Le catéchisme romain*, on this point, without giving citations from the Fathers.

57. *Div. Insts.*, Bk. II, chap. 14, §§ 1–5, pp. 162–163.

58. *The Works of Lactantius, ANCL*, i, 100.

59. *Div. Insts.*, Bk. II, chap. 8, §§ 3–5, p. 129. 'produxit similem sui spiritum, qui esset uirtutibus patris dei praeditus. . . . deinde fecit alterum, in quo indoles diuinae stirpis non permansit. itaque suapte inuidia tamquam ueneno infectus est et ex bono ad malum transcendit suoque arbitrio, quod illi a deo liberum fuerat datum, contrarium sibi nomen adsciuit. unde apparet cunctorum malorum fontem esse liuorem. inuidit enim illi antecessori suo, qui deo patri perseuerando cum probatus tum etiam carus est.'

60. *Ibid.*, chap. 12, § 17, p. 158. 'tum criminator ille inuidens operibus dei omnes fallacias et calliditates suas ad deiciendum hominem intendit, ut ei adimeret inmortalitatem.'

61. *Epitome*, chap. 22 (27), §§ 3–8, p. 694. 'tum serpens, qui erat unus ex dei ministris, inuidens homini, quod esset immortalis effectus, inlexit eum dolo ut mandatum dei legemque transcenderet. . . . serpens

uero ille, qui de factis diabolus id est criminator
siue delator nomen accepit, non destitit semen
hominis, quem a principio deceperat, persequi.
denique eum qui primus in hoc orbe generatus est,
inspirato liuore in caedem fratris armauit, ut de
duobus primogenitis hominibus alterum extingue-
ret, alterum faceret parricidam. nec quieuit dein-
ceps quominus per singulas generationes pectoribus
hominum malitiae uirus infunderet, corrumperet
deprauaret, tantis denique sceleribus obrueret, ut
iustitiae iam rarum esset exemplum, sed uiuerent
homines ritu beluarum.'

62. See Appendix D.

63. *P. L.*, Bks. I–II (ed. A. W. Verity, Cambridge,
1893), p. 96 'That the word was the title of
some evil demon is now generally held; and I suspect that in making him one of the fallen angels,
Milton simply followed some tradition of the mediaeval demonologists, though I cannot (as I had
hoped to) discover the name in Schleible's
"Kloster."'

64. See p. 64.

65. T. Newton, *Works* (London, 1782), i, 496. Newton
quotes Lactantius on Antichrist, *Div. Insts.*, Bk.
VII, chap. 19, § 6, p. 645.
Ibid., i, 723, 731. Quotes Lactantius on the millen-
nium, translating in part Bk. VII, chap. 14, §§ 9, 11,
p. 629; chap. 24, §§ 2, 5, pp. 658–659; chap. 26, § 1,
5–6, 8, pp. 665–666.

66. *P. R.* (ed. T. Newton, London, 1773), i, p. iv.
'I have been farther strengthen'd by some new

recruits, which were the more unexpected, as they were sent me from gentlemen, with whom I never had the pleasure of a personal acquaintance. . . . The reverend Mr. Calton of Marton in Lincolnshire hath contributed much more to my assistance: he favor'd me with a long correspondence; and I am at a loss which to commend most, his candor as a friend, or his penetration and learning as a critic and divine.'

67. *Ibid.*, i, 45; *P. R.*, i, 460.

68. *Ibid.*, i, 162; *P. R.*, iv, 191.

69. *Ibid.*, i, 16; *P. R.*, i, 163.

70. *Ibid.*, i, 56; *P. R.*, ii, 60.

71. *Ibid.*, i, 16; *P. R.*, i, 163.

72. *Ibid.*, i, 17. 'Hunc tamen solum primogenitum divini nominis appellatione dignatus est, patria scilicet *virtute*, ac majestate pollentem. Esse autem summi Dei filium, qui sit potestate maxima praeditus, non tantum voces prophetarum, sed etiam Sibyllarum vaticinia demonstrant. Lactantius, *Div. Inst.*, Lib. iv. 6. Cum igitur a prophetis idem manus Dei, et *virtus*, et sermo dicatur. ibid., 29.'

The exact passages are Bk. IV, chap. 6, §§ 2-4, p. 286, and chap. 29, § 6, p. 392.

73. The exact passage is Bk. II, chap. 16, § 14, p. 170.

74. *Transactions of the Connecticut Academy of Arts and Sciences*, xv (1909), 350.

75. *Div. Insts.*, Bk. II, chap. 16, § 13, p. 170.

76. The influence of Plutarch on Milton's passages treating of oracles has been dealt with briefly by Mr. C. G. Osgood, in *The Classical Mythology of*

Milton's English Poems, in Yale Studies in English, viii (1900), p. xlvi. Mr. Osgood notes the parallel between Milton's 'The oracles are dumb,' from the *Hymn on the Morning of Christ's Nativity*, 173, and section 38 of the *De defectu oraculorum*. He gives no more specific citation from Plutarch, but it is doubtless the words ἀπαυδᾶν τὰ μαντεῖα that he refers to as being quoted by Milton. Another striking parallel, occurring in section 44, is not mentioned by Mr. Osgood: ἐν δ' Ὀρχομενῷ λέγουσι . . . τὸ δὲ τοῦ Τειρεσίου χρηστήριον ἐκλιπεῖν παντάπασι καὶ μέχρι τοῦ νῦν ἀργὸν διαμένειν καὶ ἄναυδον. Plutarch, *Moralia* (ed. G. Bernardakis, Leipzig, 1891), iii, 131.

77. T. Newton, *op. cit.*, i, 321.

78. *Div. Insts.*, Bk. VII, chap. 14, § 9 (in part), p. 629.

79. See n. 65 above.

80. Milton, *Poetical Works* (ed. H. J. Todd, London, 1842).

81. Milton, *Poetical Works* (ed. Sir E. Brydges, London, 1842).

82. Milton, *Poetical Works* (ed. D. Masson, London, 1890), iii, 419.

83. A. Deuerling, *Luctatii Placidi Grammatici Glossae* (Leipzig, 1875), p. viii. 'Hermannus quoque *Schottky* in disputatione de pretio Lactantiani in Thebaidem commentarii Placidum quinto saeculo post Christum uixisse argumentis confirmauit.'

84. *P. L.*, Bks. I–II (ed. A. W. Verity, Cambridge, 1893), p. 132. 'Said to be first mentioned by name by Lactantius (fourth cent. A.D.).'

85. *P. L.* (ed. R. Bentley, London, 1732), p. 72. '*Lucan's* famous Witch *Erectho* threatens the Infernal

Powers . . . that she would call upon some Being, "at whose Name the Earth always trembled. Quo numquam terra citato Non concussa tremit." But no antient Poet ever names that Being. *Boccace*, I suppose, was the first, that invented this silly Word *Demogorgon:* which our Spenser borrow'd of him, iv. 2. 17. . . . But it is below the Dignity of this Poem to mix Barbarous Names with those of Antiquity. Let the Editor take it back to him; and the Verse be join'd, as the true Poet gave it;

Orcus and Hades; Rumor next and Chance.'

86. *P. L.* (ed. T. Newton, London, 1757), i, 168.
87. See n. 12 above.
88. A. F. Leach, 'Milton as Schoolboy and School-master,' *Proceedings of British Academy* (1907–08), pp. 295 ff.
89. See Appendix E.
90. D. Masson, *Life of Milton* (London, 1881), i, 84.
91. See pp. 103–109.
92. A. S. Cook, 'Two Notes on Milton,' *Modern Language Review*, ii (1906–07), 121.
93. See Appendix E.

IV

1. J. H. Hanford, 'The Chronology of Milton's Private Studies,' 265.
2. *Prose Works*, ii, 385. The exact passages, according to Brandt's numbering, are *Div. Insts.*, Bk. II, chap. 6, § 7, p. 122, and chap. 7, §§ 2, 4, pp. 124–125.

3. C. Sigonio, *Historiarum de occidentali imperio libri XX* (Frankfort, 1593), p. 49. 'Decennalibus actis inde Crispum Caesarem in Galliam ad limitem Rheni tutandum misit, datis magistris, qui iuvenem et in re bellica regerent et in omnibus liberalibus artibus erudirent. quorum unus fuit Lactantius Firmianus, vir disertissimus.'

4. W. T. Hale, *Of Reformation*, Yale Studies in English (New York: Henry Holt, 1916), liv, 127.

5. E. Gibbon, *Decline and Fall of the Roman Empire* (London, 1820), iii, chap. 18, p. 106. 'Crispus, the eldest son of Constantine, and the presumptive heir of the empire, is represented by impartial historians as an amiable and accomplished youth. The care of his education, or at least of his studies, was entrusted to Lactantius, the most eloquent of the christians; a preceptor admirably qualified to form the taste, and to excite the virtues, of his illustrious disciple.'

6. *Commonplace Book*, p. 24 (p. 181 of Milton's paging). 'At Constantinus petentibus Donatistis ut judices controversiis inter se et Carthaginis episcopum ortis daret, religiosissime respondit, petitis à me in seculo judicium cum ego ipse Cristi expectem judicium. Sigon. de occid. imp. l. 3.'

7. C. Sigonio, *op. cit.*, p. 44.

8. *Prose Works*, ii, 384.

9. W. T. Hale, *Of Reformation*, p. 127.

10. *Prose Works*, iii, 417. The passage quoted is from *Div. Insts.*, Bk. VI, chap. 23, § 33, p. 569.

11. *Prose Works*, iii, 415 ff. See p. 13.

12. See p. 106.
13. *Div. Insts.*:
      Bk. II,   chap. 1, §§ 15–19, p. 98.
                       9, §§ 24–26, p. 146.
                    17, § 9, p. 173.
                    18, §§ 1, 5–6, pp. 174–175.
      Bk. III, chap. 10, §§ 10–15, p. 203.
                    12, §§ 26–27, p. 211.
                    20, §§ 10–11, p. 246.
                    27, § 16, p. 263.
                    28, § 16, p. 266.
      Bk. IV,   chap. 1, § 4, p. 275.
      Bk. VII, chap. 5, §§ 6, 19–22, pp. 597, 600.
                    9, § 11, p. 612.
  Epitome, chap. 20 (25), §§ 9–10, p. 692.
              65 (70), § 4, p. 754.
  De Opificio Dei, chap. 8, §§ 2–3, p. 27.
  De Ira Dei, chap. 7, §§ 3–6, p. 78.
            14, § 2, p. 104.
            20, §§ 10–11, p. 120.
14. *Div. Insts.*, Bk. II, chap. 1, §§ 15–18, p. 98.
15. *Metamorphoses*:
    i, 76–78, quoted in *Div. Insts.*, Bk. II, chap. 8, § 64, p. 140.
    i, 79, quoted in *Div. Insts.*, Bk. I, chap. 5, § 13, p. 15; in Bk. II, chap. 5, § 2, p. 114, and in *Epitome*, chap. 3, § 5, p. 678.
    i, 84–86, quoted in *Div. Insts.*, Bk. II, chap. 1, § 15, p. 98.
16. *Metamorphoses*, i, 76–88.
17. Milton, *Poetical Works* (ed. P. H., London, 1695) 'Annotations,' p. 226.

18. Minucius Felix, *Octavius* (ed. A. Valmaggi, Genoa), p. 18. 'Praecipue cum a feris beluis hoc differamus, quod illa prona in terramque vergentia nihil nata sint prospicere nisi pabulum, nos, quibus vultus erectus, quibus suspectus in caelum datus est, sermo ac ratio, per quae Deum adgnoscimus, sentimus, imitamur, ignorare nec fas nec licet ingerentem sese oculis et sensibus nostris caelestem claritatem.'

19. *Elegia Quarta*, 43–44.

20. A. S. Cook, 'Notes on Milton's Ode on the Morning of Christ's Nativity,' *Transactions of the Connecticut Academy of Arts and Sciences*, xv (1909), 314, 323, 333–334, 349–350, 356–357, 362, 364.

21. A. S. Cook, 'Two Notes on Milton,' *Modern Language Review*, ii (1906–07), 121.

22. A. F. Leach, 'Milton as Schoolboy and Schoolmaster,' *Proceedings of the British Academy* (1907–08), pp. 309–312.

23. G. Sigerson, *The Easter Song being the First Epic of Christendom* (Dublin: The Talbot Press, 1922), p. 172.

24. *Ibid.*, p. 167.

25. *Ibid.*, p. 149.

26. *Ibid.*, p. 174. 'It is acknowledged that *Paradise Regained* is a failure, and several reasons are obvious and have been stated. One, which I consider the most important, was unknown, and that is that Milton had found but one precedent, and consequently had to fill out the simple and sufficient structure of Sedulius with interminable speeches, of

which Satan's alone formed more than half the poem.'

27. *Comus*, 463–469.
28. *Div. Insts.*, Bk. VII, chap. 20, §§ 8–9, p. 649. (Italics mine.)
29. *Aeneid*, Bk. VI, 735–740.
30. J. L. Lowes, 'The Second Nun's Prologue, Alanus, and Macrobius,' *Modern Philology*, xv, 198.
31. B. Jowett, *The Dialogues of Plato* (Oxford, 1871), i, 429.
32. *Comus*, ll. 470–472.
33. Cf. B. Jowett, *Dialogues of Plato*, i, 524–525, for higher and lower conceptions of love.
34. *Div. Insts.*, Bk. V, chap. 18, § 9, p. 459.
35. Job, 38, 4.
36. *P. L.*, viii, 167–178.
37. *Div. Insts.*, Bk. II, chap. 5, §§ 2–3, p. 114.
38. *Ibid.*, chap. 8, §§ 69, 71, p. 142.
39. A. F. Leach, *op. cit.*, p. 308.
40. *Div. Insts.*: Bk. II,   chap. 11, §§ 19–20, p. 155.
    Bk. III, chap. 20, § 2, p. 245.
    Bk. VII, chap. 2, §§ 7–9, p. 587.
41. *Commonplace Book*, p. 6 (p. 55 of Milton's paging).
42. J. H. Hanford, *op. cit.*, p. 261.
43. *Eusebii Pamphili, Ruffini, Socratis, Theodoriti, Sozomeni, Theodori, Euagrii, et Dorothei Ecclesiastica Historia* (Basle, 1611), p. 142.
44. *Ibid.* p. 228.
45. *P. L.*, viii, 415–429.
46. *De Doctrina Christiana*, p. 60.
47. *Div. Insts.*, Bk. I, chap. 8, §§ 5–7, p. 30.

48. That this notion, apparently so foreign to us, is not confined to those who have dealt with patristic thought is shown by my father's having overheard my sister say, as a three-year-old, 'I must tell Mrs. God about it.'

49. *Div. Insts.*, Bk. IV, chap. 8, § 3, p. 295.

50. *Ibid.*, Bk. I, chap. 16, §§ 16–17, p. 63.

51. *The Writings of Lactantius*, *ANCL*, i, p. x.

52. A. F. Leach, *op. cit.*, p. 307.

53. *Ibid.*

54. A. Harnack, *History of Dogma* (3d German ed., trans. N. Buchanan, Boston: Little, Brown, 1901), iv, 15–19.

55. *Writings of Lactantius*, *ANCL*, i, 222.

56. Catholic Encyclopedia (Encyclopedia Press, 1913), i, 707, 'Arianism.'

57. *Div. Insts.*, Bk. II, chap. 8, § 3, p. 129.

58. *Ibid.*, Bk. IV, chap. 6, §§ 1–2, p. 286.

59. *Ibid.*, chap. 7, § 1, p. 291. 'Fortasse quaerat aliquis hoc loco, quis sit iste tam potens, tam deo carus, et quod nomen habeat, cuius prima natiuitas non modo antecesserit mundum, uerum etiam prudentia disposuerit, uirtute construxerit.'

60. L. E. Dupin, *Nouvelle bibliothèque des auteurs ecclésiastiques* (Paris, 1693), i, 209.

61. Catholic Encyclopedia, i, 710, 'Arianism.' 'In the form which it (i.e., the heresy) took under Arius, Eusebius of Caesarea, and Eunomius, it has never been revived. Individuals, among whom are Milton and Sir Isaac Newton, were perhaps tainted with it.'

62. Psalms, 2, 7.

63. *Milton's Poetical Works* (ed. D. Masson, London, 1890), iii, 473.

64. D. Saurat, *La pensée de Milton*, p. 245.

65. See p. 159.

66. R. H. Charles, *The Book of Enoch* (2d ed., Oxford: Clarendon Press, 1912), p. 93.

67. *Ibid.*, chap. 48, § 3, p. 93.

68. *Ibid.*, § 6, p. 94.

69. *Ibid.*, chap. 52, § 7, p. 124.

70. *Pesikta Rabbati* (ed. Friedmann, Vienna, 1880), p. 161.

71. H. F. Fletcher, *Milton's Semitic Studies* (University of Chicago Press, 1926).

72. *P. L.*, iii, 383.

73. *De Doctrina Christiana*, p. 58.

74. *Ibid.*, p. 95.

75. Catholic Encyclopedia, xv, 54.

76. Migne, *Patrologiae Graecae*, xxxi, 477.

77. *Ibid.*, 'Διὰ τί Λόγος; "Ινα δειχθῇ, ὅτι ἐκ τοῦ νοῦ προῆλθε.'

78. *P. L.*, iii, 372–373.

79. John, 1, 1.

80. *De Doctrina Christiana*, p. 80.

81. *Div. Insts.*, Bk. IV, chap. 8, §§ 7–9, 11–12, pp. 296–297.

82. *The Writings of Lactantius*, *ANCL*, i, 225.

83. *Div. Insts.*, Bk. V, chaps. 11–13, pp. 433–443.

84. *Ibid.*, chap. 18, §§ 14–16, p. 460.

85. *Ibid.*, Bk. VI, chap. 20, §§ 18–22, p. 558.

86. *Ibid.*, §§ 12–13, pp. 557–558.

87. *Ibid.*, §§ 27–29, p. 560.

88. See Appendix A, 6.
89. See p. 38.
90. *Div. Insts.*, Bk. VI, chap. 21, pp. 562–563.
91. Pages 1 (p. 4 of Milton's paging), 50 (p. 241 of Milton's paging).
92. See p. 38.
93. *Tertullianus* (ed. F. Oehler, Leipzig, 1853), i, 55.
94. *Ibid.*, p. 57. 'Sed tragoedo vociferante exclamationes ille alicuius prophetae retractabit? et inter effeminati histrionis modos psalmum secum comminiscetur?'
95. A. F. Leach, *op. cit.*, p. 308.
96. H. F. Fletcher, *Milton's Semitic Studies*, p. 15. 'His actual contacts with Semitics at Cambridge may only be conjectured; but the college Latin exercise *De Idea Platonica Quemadmodum Aristoteles Intellexit*, containing the reference to Hermes Trismegistus, is further evidence of his Cambrian contact with Oriental lore and reading.'
97. *Hermetica, the Ancient Greek and Latin Writings which Contain Religious or Philosophical Teachings Ascribed to Hermes Trismegistus* (ed. W. Scott, Oxford: Clarendon Press, 1924), i, 4. 'Greeks, from the time of Herodotus or earlier, had been accustomed to translate the Egyptian god-name Thoth by the name Hermes. At a later time they distinguished this Egyptian Hermes from the very different Hermes of Greece by tacking on to the name a translation of an epithet applied by Egyptians to their god Thoth, and meaning "very great"; and thenceforward they called this personage (whether

regarded by them as a god or as a man) Hermes
τρισμέγιστος, and the Egyptian books ascribed to
him "the writings of Hermes Trismegistus." '

98. Lactantius, *CSEL*, xxvii. 2. 2, pp. 254–255.

99. *Div. Insts.*, Bk. I, chap. 6, §§ 3–4, p. 19. 'idem op-
pidum condidit, quod etiam nunc graece uocatur
Mercurii ciuitas, et Pheneatae colunt eum religiose.
qui tametsi homo fuit, antiquissimus tamen et in-
structissimus omni genere doctrinae adeo, ut ei
multarum rerum et artium scientia Trismegisto
cognomen inponeret. hic scripsit libros et quidem
multos ad cognitionem diuinarum rerum perti-
nentes, in quibus maiestatem summi ac singularis
dei asserit isdemque nominibus appellat quibus
nos "dominum et patrem." '

100. *Hermetica*, i, 8.

101. *Ibid.*, pp. 1–5.

102. *Ibid.*, p. 3.

103. *Ibid.*, p. 5.

104. See n. 95 above.

105. Tertullian, *Liber adversus Valentinianos*, chap. 15,
in Migne, *Patrologiae Cursus Completus*, ii, 567.

106. Clement of Alexandria, *Stromata*, Bk. VI, chap. 4,
in Migne, *Patrologiae Graecae*, ix, 252–256.

107. Augustine, *De Civitate Dei*, Bk. VIII, chaps. 23–
24, 26.

108. *Stromata*, in *Commonplace Book*, p. 8 (p. 71 of
Milton's paging).
De Civitate Dei, in *Commonplace Book*, p. 39 (p. 195
of Milton's paging).

109. Cicero, *De Natura Deorum*, Bk. III, chap. 22. 'Mercurius . . . quintus, quem colunt Pheneatae, qui Argum dicitur interemisse, ob eamque causam Aegyptum profugisse atque Aegyptiis leges et litteras tradidisse. Hunc Aegyptii Theuth appellant, eodemque nomine anni primus mensis apud eos vocatur.'

110. J. H. Hanford, *Chronology of Milton's Private Studies*, p. 290, n. 155.

111. L. Thorndike, *A History of Magic and Experimental Science during the First Thirteen Centuries of our Era* (New York: Macmillan, 1923), i, 287.

112. *Ibid.*, ii, chap. 45, pp. 214–228.

113. F. Bacon, *Of the Advancement of Learning* (Everyman ed.), p. 3. 'There is met in your Majesty a rare conjunction as well of divine and sacred literature, as of profane and human; so as your Majesty standeth invested of that triplicity, which in great veneration was ascribed to the ancient Hermes; the power and fortune of a king, the knowledge and illumination of a priest, and the learning and universality of a philosopher.'

114. *Purchas his Pilgrimage* (London, 1617), Bk. VI, chap. 3, § 2, p. 724.

115. *Div. Insts.*, Bk. II, chap. 3, § 5, p. 104.

116. *Ibid.*, chap. 1, § 5, p. 96.

117. S. Brandt, 'Zum Phoenix des Lactantius,' *Rheinisches Museum für Philologie*, xlvii (1892), 390.

118. The following editions of the sixteenth and seventeenth centuries contain the *De Ave Phoenice:*
    Venice: Joannes Tacuinus de Tridino, 1502.

Florence: Iuntina, 1513.
Paris: Petit, 1513.
Venice: Aldus Manutius, 1515; 1535.
Lyons: Tornaesius and Gazeius, 1556.
Basle: Xystus Betuleius, 1563.
Anvers: Thomasius, 1570.
Leyden: Gallaeus, 1660.

The references for the editions of Betuleius and Thomasius are from *Claudii Claudiani Opera* (Amsterdam, 1760), p. 1035.

119. *Epitaphium Damonis*, 185–189 (see p. 124); *P. L.*, v, 272–274; *S. A.*, 1699–1707.

120. *De Ave Phoenice*, 125–144.

121. *Ibid.*, 133.

122. *CSEL*, xxvii. ii. 2, 261–262.

123. Claudian, *De Consulatu Stilichonis*, ii, 414–417.

124. M. Manitius, *Geschichte der christlich-lateinischen Poesie des achten Jahrhunderts* (Stuttgart, 1891), p. 49.

125. Claudian, *Epigram de Phoenice*, 21.

126. Pliny, *Naturalis Historia*, Bk. X, chap. 2.

127. C. G. Osgood, *The Classical Mythology of Milton's English Poems*, p. 70, 'Phoenix.'

128. Herodotus, Bk. II, 73.

129. Claudian, *Epigram de Phoenice*, 45–47.

NOTES

APPENDICES

C

1. *Commonplace Book*, p. 3 (p. 13 of Milton's paging).
2. S. Purchas, *Purchas his Pilgrimes* (London, 1625), i, Bk. III, chap. 1, § 5, p. '132' (following p. 121).
3. *Commonplace Book*, p. 6 (p. 57 of Milton's paging).
4. J. H. Hanford, 'The Chronology of Milton's Private Studies,' *Publications of the Modern Language Association*, xxxvi (1921), p. 275.
5. *Purchas his Pilgrimes*, ii, Bk. VI, chap. 1, § 1, p. 759.
6. *Ibid.*, p. 795.
7. See n. 32 of chapter III above.
8. See *Ibid.*, n. 31.
9. *Purchas his Pilgrimage* (London, 1617), Bk. I, chap. 17, p. 90.
10. *Ibid.*, p. 89.
11. A. S. Cook, 'Notes on Milton's Nativity Ode,' *Transactions of the Connecticut Academy of Arts and Sciences*, xv (1909), 356.
12. (Pseudo-) Lucian, Περὶ τῆς Συρίης Θεοῦ, § 4.
13. *P. L.*, Bk. I (ed. J. Callander, Glasgow, 1750), p. 79.
14. *Purchas his Pilgrimage*, Bk. I, chap. 17, p. 90.
15. (Pseudo-) Lucian, Περὶ τῆς Συρίης Θεοῦ, §§ 6–8.
16. See n. 4 above.
17. *Purchas his Pilgrimage*, Bk. V, chap. 3, § 1, p. 721.

D

1. *The Book of Enoch* (ed. R. H. Charles, Oxford, 1912), Appendix I, p. 278, Syncellus' fragment. καὶ ταῦτα τὰ ὀνόματα τῶν ἀρχόντων αὐτῶν· α′ Σεμιαζᾶς, ὁ ἄρχων αυτῶν. β′ Ἀταρκούφ. γ′ Ἀρακιήλ. δ′ Χωβαβιήλ. ε′ Ὁραμμαμή. ϛ′ Ῥαμιήλ. ζ′ Σαμψίχ. ἡ Ζακιήλ. θ′ Βαλκιήλ. ι′ Ἀζαλζήλ. ια′ Φαρμαρός. ιβ′ Ἀμαριήλ. ιγ′ Ἀναγημάς. ιδ′ Θαυσαήλ. ιε′ Σαμιήλ. ιϛ′ Σαρινᾶς. ιζ′ Εὐμιήλ. ιη′ Τυριήλ. ιθ′ Ἰουμιήλ. κ′ Σαριήλ.

2. *Ibid.*, p. 18, chap. 8 (trans. R. H. Charles). 'And Azâzêl taught men to make swords, and knives, and shields, and breastplates, and made known to them the metals and the art of working them, and bracelets, and ornaments, and the use of antimony, and the beautifying of the eyelids, and all kinds of costly stones, and all colouring tinctures.'

3. *P. L.*, i (ed. J. Callander, Glasgow, 1750), p. 110.

4. D. Saurat, *La pensée de Milton*, pp. 241–246. Professor Saurat could not have known Callander's work on this point, or he would not have called Newton 'le plus informé de ces questions,' on p. 239.

5. *Book of Enoch*, chap. 6, § 1, p. 13 — chap. 7, § 3, p. 18

6. *P. L.*, xi, 646–659.
   Book of Enoch, chap. 7, §§ 3–6, p. 18.

7. *P. L.*, xi, 610–613.
   Book of Enoch, chap. 8, §§ 1–3, pp. 18–19.

8. *Ibid.*, pp. 20–22, chap. 9, §§ 1–11.

9. D. Saurat, *op. cit.*, p. 237.

E

1. '*Sic*, for *hominis*': J. H. Lupton.
2. J. H. Lupton, *A Life of John Colet, D.D.* (London, 1887), p. 279.
3. Milton, *Poems upon Several Occasions* (ed. T. Warton, London, 1785), p. 90. 'Milton was educated at saint Paul's school, contiguous to the church; and thus became impressed with an early reverence for the solemnities of the antient ecclesiastical architecture, its vaults, shrines, iles, pillars, and painted glass, rendered yet more aweful by the accompaniment of the choral service.'
   A. F. Leach, 'Milton as Schoolboy and Schoolmaster,' *Proceedings of the British Academy* (1907–08), p. 299. 'It is certain that the *genius loci* had its effect on his mind. For it was not at Cambridge or at Horton parish church, but as a boy of St. Paul's School, attending St. Paul's Cathedral, that he learned to
       love the high embowèd roof,
       With antique pillars massy proof,
       And storied windows richly dight,
       Casting a dim religious light' . . .
4. *Il Penseroso*, ll. 155–166.
   On the Morning of Christ's Nativity, ll. 130–132.
5. Erasmus, *The Lives of Jehan Vitrier and John Colet* (ed. J. H. Lupton, London, 1883), p. 27. 'At his (i.e. Colet's) father's death he had inherited a large sum of money; and fearing lest, if he hoarded it up, it might breed some distemper of mind in

him, he built with it in St. Paul's Churchyard a
new school of splendid structure, dedicated to the
Child Jesus.'

6. *Ibid*.

7. *Ibid*., p. 52. 'The original service in the school
chapel was replaced after the Reformation by a
form of Latin prayers, in which the "Capellanus"
and "Chorus" took part alternately. The custom
of late years has been for the captain of the school
to read a selection of these prayers at the beginning
and end of morning and afternoon school.'

8. *Preces Hymni et Catechismus Graece et Latine in
usum antiquae et celebris Scholae S. Pauli apud
Londinates* (new ed., London, 1896), p. 18.

9. J. H. Lupton, *Life of Colet*, p. 152, n. 1.

10. *Preces Hymni et Catechismus*, p. 22.

BIBLIOGRAPHY

BIBLIOGRAPHY

PRIMARY SOURCES

Lactantius

Opera omnia (ed. S. Brandt and G. Laubmann, Vienna, 1890–97), in *Corpus Scriptorum Ecclesiasticorum Latinorum*, vols. xix; xxvii, ii, 1; xxvii, ii, 2.

Works (trans. W. Fletcher, Edinburgh, 1871), in *Ante-Nicene Christian Library*, xxi, xxii.

J. P. Migne, *Patrologiae Cursus Completus* (Paris, 1844–64).

Milton

Poetical Works (ed. D. Masson, London, 1890).

Prose Works (ed. H. G. Bohn, London, 1848–52).

Commonplace Book (ed. A. J. Horwood: Camden Society, 1876).

De Doctrina Christiana (ed. C. R. Sumner, Cambridge, 1825).

Of Reformation in England (ed. W. T. Hale, New Haven, 1916), Yale Studies in English, vol. liv.

SECONDARY SOURCES

Lactantius

O. Bardenhewer, *Geschichte der altkirchlichen Literatur* (Freiburg: Herder, 1903).

S. Brandt, 'Zum Phoenix des Lactantius,' *Rheinisches Museum für Philologie*, xxvii (1892), 390 ff.

C. T. Cruttwell, *A Literary History of Early Christianity* (London, 1893).

R. Pichon, *Lactance, étude sur le mouvement philosophique et religieux sous le règne de Constantin* (Paris, 1901).

A. Riese, 'Über den Phoenix des Lactantius,' *Rheinisches Museum für Philologie*, xxxi (1876), 446 ff.

Catholic Encyclopedia (New York: Appleton, 1910), viii, 736, 'Lactantius.'

Encyclopædia Britannica (11th ed., Cambridge: University Press, 1911), xvi, 55, 'Lactantius.'

Dictionary of Christian Biography (ed. Smith and Wace, London, 1882), iii, 613, 'Lactantius.'

Milton

A. S. Cook, 'Two Notes on Milton: I. The Ode on the Nativity and the Poems of Mantuan,' *Modern Language Review*, ii (1906–07), 121 ff.
'Notes on Milton's Ode on the Morning of Christ's Nativity,' *Transactions of the Connecticut Academy of Arts and Sciences*, xv (1909), 307 ff.

J. H. Hanford, 'The Chronology of Milton's Private Studies,' *Publications of the Modern Language Association*, xxxvi (1921), 251 ff.

A. F. Leach, 'Milton as Schoolboy and Schoolmaster,' *Proceedings of the British Academy* (1907–08), pp. 295 ff.

L. E. Lockwood, *Lexicon to the English Poetical Works of John Milton* (New York: Macmillan, 1907).

D. Masson, *Life of Milton* (1st ed., London, 1859–80).

M. F. J. McDonnell, *The History of St. Paul's School* (London: Chapman and Hall, 1909).

C. G. Osgood, *The Classical Mythology of Milton's English Poems* (New York: Henry Holt, 1900), Yale Studies in English, vol. viii.

P. Pritchard, *The Influence of the Fathers upon Milton, with Especial Reference to Augustine* (Cornell University, 1925).

D. Saurat, *La pensée de Milton* (Paris: F. Alcan, 1920).

INDEX

INDEX

Abdiel, 101
Adam, 59, 92, 100
Adonis, 154, 155
Aelian, 51
Aeschylus, 54
Ambrose, 5, 47, 74
Ammon, 117
Ammonius, 118
Angels,
  fallen angels, 52
  nature of, 52
  foreknowledge of man, 57
  jealousy of man, 57, 60
  fall of, 58
  sin with women, 58, 59
Antiquitarians, 8
Apis, 53, 54
Arius, 93
Arnobius, 40, 43, 51
Asclepius, 117
Ashtoreth, 153, 154
Athanasius, 5, 47, 61, 72
Athenagoras, 58
Augustine, 5, 15, 47, 51, 58, 59,
  61, 74, 119, 120
  De Civitate Dei, 119
Azazel, 60, 158

Bacon, Francis, 120, 199 n. 113
Baptista Mantuanus, 68, 80, 81
Basil, 5, 47, 72, 73, 108
  *Homilia in illud, in Principio
  erat Verbum*, 108
Bentley, R., 49, 50, 61, 66
  Paradise Lost, 49
  *Dissertation upon the Epistles of
  Phalaris*, 50

Letter to Mill, 50
*Proposals for Printing a New
  Edition of the Greek Testa-
  ment*, 50
Bible, 4, 14, 82, 166
Boccaccio, 49, 66
  Genealogiae Deorum, 49
Book of Enoch, 58, 102, 103, 118,
  158, 159, 202 nn. 1, 2
Brandt, S., vi, vii, 116, 126
Brydges, Sir E., 65
Buckingham, Countess of, 5
Buckingham, Duke of, 5

Callander, J., of Craigforth, 50,
  51, 52, 53, 54, 55, 56, 57, 58,
  60, 61, 65, 67, 158
Calton, 61, 62, 63, 64, 65, 67
Cambridge, 79, 115, 116
Catholic Encyclopedia, 98, 99, 108
Caxton, Wm., *Recuyell of the
  Historyes of Troye*, 49
Charles, R. H., 102
Chaucer, 85
  Second Nun's Prologue, 85
Christ (*see also* Jesus), 59, 62, 68,
  74, 82, 83, 96, 97, 110, 116,
  161, 163, 164, 165, 166
  Son of God, 58, 59, 62, 98, 99,
  100, 101, 102, 105, 106, 107,
  109
Λόγος, 108, 109
Chrysostom, 5, 34, 47
Cicero, 40, 41, 119, 121, 199 n.
  109
Claudian, 127, 128, 129, 130, 131,
  132

De Consulatu Stilichonis, *II*, 128

Epigram de Phoenice, 128

Clement of Alexandria, 6, 20, 51, 119

Colet, J., v, 67, 68, 80, 81, 82, 119

Constantine, 13, 70, 71, 93

Cook, A. S., 63, 68, 80, 154

Cyprian, 5, 40, 43, 58, 72, 108

Cyril of Alexandria, 5

Daniel, 53, 118

Dante, 109

Demogorgon, 65, 66

Dictionary of Christian Biography, 99

Donatists, 71

Dupin, L. E., 99

Ennius, 48, 51, 57

Epicurus, 25

Epiphanius, 5, 73

Erasmus, *The Lives of Jehan Vitrier and John Colet*, 163

Euhemerus, 48, 57

Euripides, 51

Eusebius, 20, 51, 92, 93, 108

'Fisher the Jesuit,' 5

Fletcher, H. F., 105, 115
   Milton's Semitic Studies, 105

Gabriel, 159

Gaia, 55

Genesis, 58

Geoffrey of Monmouth, 36, 178 n. 41

Gibbon, E., 71, 191 n. 5

Gregory Nazianzen, 5, 44

Gregory of Nyssa, 5, 108

Hale, W. T., 9, 71, 72

Hall, J., *Humble Remonstrance*, 8

Hanford, J. H., 16, 20, 22, 23, 34, 36, 70, 119, 151

Harnack, 97

Hermes, 116

Hermes Trismegistus, 68, 115, 116, 117, 118, 119, 120, 121

Hermetica, etc., 197 n. 97

Herodotus, 129

Hesiod, 47, 48, 53, 54, 181 n. 11

Hilary, 5

Homer, 54, 56

Horace, 53

Hume, Patrick, 46, 47, 48, 77

Ignatius, 7, 15, 16, 20
   Epistle to the Philadelphians, 15

Irenaeus, 5, 7, 57, 58

Jerome, 5, 47, 51, 53, 74, 185 n. 38

Jesus (*see also* Christ), 163, 164, 165

Job, 89

John of Damascus, 5

Jortin, 66, 67

Jove, 57

Jowett, B., *The Dialogues of Plato*, 'Phaedo,' 32, 86

Judgement of Dr. Rainoldes, 172 n.7

Juno, 48

Jupiter, 48, 49, 56

Justin Martyr, 5, 13, 15, 16, 51, 58, 61, 62, 63, 73, 108, 119, 121

   First Apology, 15, 17

   Second Apology, 15, 17

Justus Jonas, 163

Lactantius,
   cited by Milton in *Commonplace Book*, 21, 34–38
   problem of evil, 21, 23, 137–141

virtue based on resistance to evil, 23–26, 31, 34, 137–141

choice between good and evil necessary for wisdom, 23, 24, 138–141

argument in a circle, 24

answer to Epicurus, 25

use of forms of *exercere*, 28

use of forms of *adversarius*, 30, 31

Seneca a probable source for, 32

problem of vengeance for a just man, 34, 141–142

paederasty, 35

importance of intelligence to man, 37, 142–144

patriotism, 38, 144, 145

drama, 39, 145, 146

answer to Lucretius' arraignment of Nature, 37

style, 42

example disproving influence of race and climate on literature, 43

attack on drama, 38, 43, 112, 113, 145, 146

theory of unworthiness of senses, 43, 146

not a great thinker, 44, 74

disregard of, by commentators on Milton, 46

account of Titan given by, 48, 147, 148

Bentley's use of, 49, 50

Callander's use of, 50, 52–57

origin of Saturn, 54, 55

partition of world, 56

Jupiter's ousting of Saturn, 56

burial of Jupiter, 57

fall of the angels, 58, 59

Arianism, 59, 97, 99–101, 105–107

Callander's incorrect attribution to, 57–58

Newton's use of, 61

Calton's use of, 61–64

a possible source for Milton's knowledge of oracles, 63

Masson's confusion with Lactantius Placidus, 66

quotation of, by Sprague, 67

use at St. Paul's School, 67, 68, 81

influence on Milton traced by Leach, 67, 68

cited by Milton in prose, 70, 72, 74

Milton's opinion of, 72

Milton's use of, in *Tetrachordon*, 72, 73

argument from man's upright posture, 75–77

use of Ovid as a source for this argument, 77

physical pain in after life, 83

virtue triumphant over adversity, 88

incomprehensibility of God, 89, 91

sexlessness of God, 93–96

audibility of Λόγος, 107–111

conception of God, 109

use of local color, 100

coupling of Roman drama and gladiatorial shows, 112, 113

effeminacy of stage, 112–113

citations of Hermes Trismegistus, 116–118

Socrates as advocate of truth, 122

stupidity of idolatry, 122, 123

problem of authorship of *De Ave Phoenice*, 123

Lactantius (*continued*)
  Ovid a source for phoenix material, 126
  a source for Claudian for phoenix material, 128, 131
  presentation of phoenix legend, 124, 125, 129, 130
  editions of, 173 n. 11

  Works

  Divinae Institutiones: Bk. I, 55, 56–57, 95, 96, 147–148; Bk. II, 52, 63, 70–71, 76, 91–92, 121–122, 123; Bk. III, 30, 31; Bk. IV, 98–99, 109–110; Bk. V, 88–89, 137–138; Bk. VI, 73, 112–113, 141–142, 144–145, 145–146, 146; Bk. VII, 84. *See also* 176 nn. 24, 27, 180 n. 61, 185 n. 43, 186 n. 59, 195 n. 59, 198 n. 99
  De Ave Phoenice, 124–125, 125, 199 n. 118
  De Ira Dei, 24, 25, 138–141
  De Opificio Dei, 142–144
  Epitome, 59, 186 n. 61
Lactantius Placidus, 66
Lake, K., viii
Laubmann, G., vi
Laud, William, 5, 169 nn. 4, 5
  conference with 'Mr. Fisher the Jesuit,' 5
Leach, A. F., vi, vii, 67, 68, 80, 81, 92, 97, 98, 100, 115, 116, 118, 203 n. 3
  'Milton as Schoolboy and Schoolmaster,' vi, 6, 7
Leo Afer, 151
Lockwood, L., *Lexicon to the English Poetical Works of John Milton*, vii
Lowes, John L., viii, 149

Lucian, 154, 156
Lucretius, 37
Luke, 165

Masson, D., 19, 20, 65, 66, 67, 68, 102
Mempricius, 36
Menander, 53
Michael, 159
Migne, J. P., vii, 16
Milton,
  knowledge of Fathers, 4
  the Bible his main authority, 4, 14, 111
  appearance of scorn toward Fathers, 6, 7
  use of Fathers against themselves, 6
  attack on opponents' use of Fathers, 6, 7
  attitude toward Bishop Hall, 8
  rejection of uncritical acceptance of Fathers, 9–12
  effect of controversy on his views on Fathers, 9
  superior knowledge of Fathers, 10
  warning against random citation of Fathers, 11, 12
  respectful treatment of Fathers, 12–14
  change in attitude toward Fathers, 14
  accuracy vindicated, 15–17
  knowledge of Lactantius, 18, 26, 33
  knowledge of Fathers doubted by Masson, 19, 20
  consideration of the problem of evil, 21
  citations of Lactantius in *Commonplace Book*, 21, 34–38

possible slips in accuracy, 21, 22, 35

possible differences in his edition of Lactantius, 21, 22, 35

way of work in *Commonplace Book*, 22

time of his entries from Lactantius, 23, 34, 36, 70

summaries of thought found in Lactantius, 23, 28, 36, 37

discovery of flaw in Lactantius' thought, 24

theory of evil as necessary for development of virtue, 27, 31

use of words possibly borrowed from Lactantius, 27–31, 33, 34, 37, 88, 123, 125, 127

possibly unconscious recollection of Lactantius, 31, 32, 111, 133

possible influence of Seneca, 32–34

recollection of details from reading, 36, 74

answer to patristic attack on drama, 39, 43, 44

comment on Tertullian's style, 39–41

opinion of Arnobius, 40

opinion of the style of Lactantius, 40

attitude toward Lactantius' attack on music, 44

bewilderment of commentators over Titan, 47, 48

meaning of 'Azazel,' 60

Lactantius a possible source of his knowledge of oracles, 63

influence of Lactantius traced by Leach, 67, 68

citations of Lactantius in prose, 70, 73, 74

knowledge of Sigonio, 71

opinion of Lactantius, 72

use of Lactantius in *Tetrachordon*, 72, 73

use of argument from upright posture, possibly from Lactantius, 75–78

Ovid a possible source of this argument, 77, 78

possible knowledge of Lactantius at St. Paul's, 79

possible knowledge of other Fathers at St. Paul's, 79–81

possible debt to Sedulius, 81–83

earliest trace of influence of Lactantius, 83–85, 88

Virgil a possible source for, 84, 85

Chaucer not a possible source for, 85

Plato a source for, 86, 87

likeness of 'fame' in *Lycidas* to Lactantian 'virtue,' 88

consideration of incomprehensibility of God possibly inspired by Lactantius, 89–93

entry from Eusebius on incomprehensibility of God, 92, 93

consideration of sexlessness of God, possibly inspired by Lactantius, 93–96

views on begetting of Son, 100, 101, 106

contradiction in announcement to angels of begetting of Son, 101, 102

possible survival of *Enoch* tradition, 102–104

consideration of audibility of Λόγος possibly inspired by Lactantius, 107–111

conception of God, 109

Milton (*continued*)

views on effeminacy of drama possibly inspired by Lactantius, 114, 115

knowledge of Hermes Trismegistus, 115–121

reference to Socrates as advocate of truth, 121

stupidity of idolatry, 122

use of phoenix legend in *Epitaphium Damonis* possibly inspired by Lactantius, 124–126, 129–132

Claudian a possible source for phoenix material, 128, 130, 131

Pliny a possible source for phoenix material, 128, 130, 131

general influence of Lactantius, 132, 133

Purchas a possible source for, 149, 153–157

knowledge of Purchas shown by *Commonplace Book*, 149–152, 156

Lucian a possible source for, 156

knowledge of Syncellus' fragment possible only after blindness, 159, 160

influence of St. Paul's School, 163, 164

conception of Boy Christ possibly influenced by prayers used at St. Paul's, 166

Works

Animadversions upon the Remonstrant's Defence against Smectymnuus, 12

Apology for Smectymnuus, 40

Areopagitica, 27, 28, 29, 30, 31, 32, 33, 74, 91, 132

A Treatise of Civil Power in Ecclesiastical Causes, 11

Commonplace Book, 4, 16, 18, 19, 20, 22, 26, 27, 28, 29, 33, 34, 36, 43, 44, 70, 71, 74, 92, 93, 108, 114, 119, 133, 137, 138, 141, 142, 144, 145, 146, 149, 156, 172 n. 7, 173 n. 10, 178 n. 5

Comus, 83, 87, 88; ll. 463–469, 83; ll. 470–472, 87

De Doctrina Christiana, 15, 94, 95, 106, 109

De Idea Platonica quemadmodum Aristoteles intellexit, ll. 32–34, 115

Epitaphium Damonis, ll. 185–189, 124, 131, 132

History of Britain, 36

Hymn on the Morning of Christ's Nativity, l. 226, 157

Il Penseroso, 115, 121; l. 88, 115

Lycidas, ll. 81–82, 88, 89

Of Prelatical Episcopacy, 14, 20

Of Reformation in England, 6, 7, 8, 15, 16, 39, 70, 72, 88

Paradise Lost: Bk. I, 47, 51, 52, 53, 54, 56, 57, 60, 153, 155, 181 n. 12, 187 n. 63; Bk. II, 65, 187 n. 63, 189 n. 85; Bk. III, 106, 181 n. 12; Bk. V, 100, 102; Bk. VII, 75, 89; Bk. VIII, 90, 91, 94; Bk. XII, 115–120, 122

Paradise Regained: Bk. I, 62, 63, 165, 187 n. 66, 188 n. 72; Bk. II, 61; Bk. IV, 112

Poems upon Several Occasions, 203 n. 3

Samson Agonistes, 44, 64, 124

Tetrachordon, 12, 14, 70, 72, 74
The Reason of Church Government Urged against Prelaty, 10
Minucius Felix, 5, 40, 42, 55, 79
Octavius, 79, 193 n. 18
Moloch, 51, 52, 153

Neptune, 48, 56
Newton, T., 61, 63, 64, 65
P. R., 61, 62
Dissertations on the Prophecies, 61

Oceanus, 67
Olaus Magnus, 51
Ops, 48
Origen, 5, 6, 47, 51, 73
'Orpheus,' 54
Osgood, C. G., *The Classical Mythology of Milton's English Poems*, 129
Ovid, 77, 78, 126, 127
Metamorphoses, 78

Pesikta Rabbati, 103, 104
Philo Byblius, 51
Phoenix, 64, 124, 125, 126, 127, 128, 129, 130, 131
Pichon, R., 41, 42
Plato, 51, 87, 88, 117, 121
Phaedo, 86
Pliny, 128, 129, 130, 132
Naturalis Historia, 128
Plutarch, *De Defectu Oraculorum*, 63
    influence of, on Milton's passages treating of oracles, 188 n. 76
Pluto, 48, 56
Pritchard, Paul, 6, 10, 15, 17, 20, 21
Prudentius, 53, 67, 68, 80, 81

Purchas, S., 51, 120, 149, 150, 151, 152, 153, 154, 156, 157
Pilgrimage, 51, 120, 152, 156, 184 n. 32
Pilgrimes, 149
Pythagoras, 117

Raphael (archangel), 92, 100, 101, 159
Richardson, J. (father and son) *Explanatory Notes and Remarks on, Milton's 'Paradise Lost'* 49

St. Paul's School, v, vi, 67, 68, 69, 79, 81, 116, 119, 121, 161, 163
Sandys, G., 51, 153, 184 n. 31
Travailes, 51
Satan, 26, 30, 58, 59, 60, 63, 101
Saturn, 48, 54, 55, 56
Saurat, D., 58, 59, 102, 158, 159, 160
La pensée de Milton, 58
Saxo Grammaticus, 51
Scott, W., 117, 118
Scripture, 7, 111
Sedulius, 68, 81, 82, 83
Carmen Paschale, 81, 82
Seneca, 32, 33, 34
De Providentia, 32
Servius, 85
Sigerson, G., 81, 82, 83
The Easter Song of Sedulius, 81, 82
Sigonio, C., 71
De Occidentali Imperio, 71
Socrates, 53, 121, 122
Socrates (church historian), 93
Solomon, 154
Statius, 66
Thebaid, 66
Stilicho, 127

'Summatra,' 149
Sybil, 57
Syncellus, G., 58, 102, 103, 158, 159, 160
   Chronographia, ab Adamo usque ad Diocletianum, 159

Tacitus, 51
Tat, 117
Tatlock, J. S. P., viii, 49
Tertullian, 5, 6, 20, 21, 22, 38, 40, 41, 42, 43, 47, 73, 114, 115, 119
   De Spectaculis, 21, 38, 114
Thammuz, 154, 156
Theodoret, 47
Thorndike, L., 119, 120
Thoth, 116
Titan, 47, 48, 49, 67
Titans, 47, 48, 67

Todd, H. J., 65
Typhon, 157

Uranus, 55
Uriel, 159
Usher, J., 19, 20
   The Judgement of Doctor Rainoldes touching the originall of Episcopacy, 19

Varro, 51
Verity, A. W., 60, 66, 67
Virgil, 84, 85
   Aeneid, 84

Wolfson, H. A., viii, 103, 104

Yalkut Shime 'oni, 104, 105
Young, Thomas, 79